Build a Better Birdhouse

Build a Better Birdhouse
(or Feeder)

New Designs in Avian Architecture

By Malcolm Wells

WILLOW CREEK PRESS
Minocqua, Wisconsin

ISBN 1-57223-049-5

Previously published by the author as:
Classic Architectural Birdhouses and Feeders
ISBN 0-9621878-0-1

Typeset and reissued in 1996 by Willow Creek Press
P.O. Box 147, Minocqua, Wisconsin 54548

For information on other Willow Creek titles,
call 1-800-850-WILD

Printed in the U.S.A.

Library of Congress Cataloging-in-Publication Data

Wells, Malcolm.
    [Classic architectural birdhouses and feeders]
    Build a better birdhouse (or feeder) : new designs
in avian architecture / by Malcolm Wells.
        p.   cm.
    Originally published : Classic architectural
birdhouses and feeders. c1988.
    ISBN 1-57223-049-5 (alk. paper)
    1. Birdhouses—Design and construction. 2. Bird
feeders—Design and construction.   I. Title.
    QL676.5.W377   1996
    690'.892—dc20   96-42406
                                          CIP

". . . all work passes directly out of the
hands of the architect into the hands of
nature, to be perfected."
— Henry D. Thoreau

Table of Contents

Introduction

When it comes to the subject of houses for humans, the styles vary from year to year, from region to region, and from fad to fad! We're not at all sure what the most appropriate shelter for *homo sapiens* should be, and our architecture expresses our uncertainty. When we move to another state — or just down the street — we aren't surprised to find houses that have nothing to do with the region in which they stand. Cape Cod cottages are seen in the Arizona desert, and ranchers are popular in Maine.

Anything goes.

And, adding to our confusion is the wide range of building materials now available to us. No longer must we fell and saw into boards the trees from which our houses will be built. We order windows from Minnesota, plasterboard from Pennsylvania, lumber from Oregon, tiles from Mexico, vinyl from Kentucky, lamps from Korea, towel bars from Illinois, and cabinets from Canada. The result: houses with all the charm of building materials showrooms.

Being no longer wild creatures, no longer partial to caves or tree huts, we sail rudderless on the sea of architecture. That's why we respond so positively to the discovery of birds' nests or animals' dens. They seem, without exception, so right, so much a part of their environment, that we can imagine no changes that would make them more so. They have an inevitability of design that makes us wish our own shelters could be as appropriate.

But it is not to be; we lost, somewhere along the way, the capacity to design, by instinct, perfect natural houses. All we can do now is hire architects and hope for the best.

Maybe it serves us right. Maybe it's the price we have to pay for the convenience of indoor plumbing and automatic heating systems. Unnatural conveniences breed unnatural surroundings.

Well, so be it. The only sad part is that we then try to impose our artificiality upon other creatures.

Take birds, for instance.

We forget that they, even the most common ones around us, are utterly wild, as wild as the lion on the Serengeti or the shark in the sea. To often, we regard birds only as cute little toys that flit from branch to branch making chirping noises. Consequently, the birdhouses we offer them are not only ugly and inappropriate, they also help perpetuate our avian misconception.

How in the world did we manage to produce nonsense like this . . .

. . . when all the messages from the natural world were sayings so richly different?

Not that the birds care, of course. They'll nest almost anywhere, in anything, when the mating pressure is on and competition for housing is hot. So you can't go by their responses to our silliness. Birds will use whatever fits, and many man-made birdhouses fit very well. That's not the problem. The problem is that we make such fools of ourselves.

We go about it all wrong.

In sixth grade shop class we were taught that six pieces of wood, with a hole in one of them, could be assembled to create a perfect birdhouse. The teacher said so; it had to be true. Our parents marveled at our ingenuity, thereby confirming what the teacher had said. We marveled at it, too. Then we hung our masterpieces out of doors and, sure enough, birds nested in them, reconfirming everything. How much more perfect could 6 pieces of wood possibly get?

Much more.

We are entering the age of environmental awareness.

No longer do we see smoke-belching
chimneys as signs of economic well-being.
No longer do we see harbors as the places
to dump our sewage, or chemicals as the way to better living. We're slowly
coming to realize that it is we who have polluted and poisoned and eroded our
earthly home, we who have wiped out thousands of species, we whose very
houses are environmental horrors, wasting resources and destroying land.

Our awakening is leading us to take a closer look at creatures we once thought
of only as sources of food, fur, feathers or song. We're beginning to discover
what awesome miracles share the land with us, and that discovery is changing
the way we see not only human architecture but the architecture we offer the
birds as well.

Obviously, though, we can never match the structures the birds themselves create. Imagine weaving a delicate basket of twigs and grasses, in just a few days, with no previous experience, no practice sessions, no tools, and no hands!

The best we can ever hope to do is build bridges — transitions — from the manmade to the wild. Then, instead of having silly-looking bird boxes embarrassing us out of doors, we can show that we've at least tried to bridge that awful chasm between the wild and the human.

dumb

Even then, we are likely to fail. At best, we can only partly succeed. But we owe it to the Creator of the Birds if not to the birds themselves to give it our very best shot: to say, somehow, in human terms, what they say so movingly in grass and twigs and straw.

What follows has to be, on that score, both an embarrassment and a failure, but it was done more out of awe than out of ornithological science, and because of that perhaps I will be forgiven.

Materials

If you live near a ghost town, or along a riverbank or a bayshore, or near a building that's being constructed or demolished, or near a lumberyard or a sawmill, you should be able to pick up a year's supply of birdhouse materials in no time. All you need look for are weathered boards of various sizes, mostly thin (1/2", 3/4" and 1" material), and poles or small tree trunks for use as mounting posts.

Ideally, you shouldn't have to pay for anything but the nails. If birds can scrounge all the materials they need, surely we well-educated, computer-assisted, tool-using geniuses can manage to round up a few pieces of scrap wood that way, too.

Just make sure the materials you collect don't smell of paint or poisons, and try to find some pieces with interesting grains. Here's your chance to use all the warped, split, beautiful rejects you've wanted to build into something.

If the nails you need come in a plastic pack, dump its contents onto the hardware store counter and ask for a paper bag. (Keep the organic movement alive; spread the word.) The materials that the birds use eventually rot and become wildflowers or trees again. When we introduce deadly, soulless materials like plastics, or paint, or preservatives, into the lifestreams of such beautiful creatures, we degrade not only them but ourselves as well.

Basic Requirements

Birdhouses and bird feeders must be reasonably safe from attack by cats, dogs, kids and gorillas.

Birdhouses must be well ventilated to help reduce the chance of severe overheating on blazing July afternoons. This is a good reason to use an earth sheltered roof.

Birdhouses must be well drained; rainstorms and unattended sprinklers can flood those that have no outlets. Water always runs downhill; you take it from there.

Birdhouses must be built in such ways that they won't fall to the ground, and yet be easy to hang, take down, open, inspect, clean, repair, and rehang. Birds don't take down, open, inspect, clean, repair and rehang their nests, but once human interference takes place it carries with it responsibility for side effects brought on by the use of artificial habitats. Birdhouses left up year after year without cleaning can become havens for all sorts of parasites and fungi. The tiny rooms can also become clogged with old nesting materials, or they can become the nests of mice or rats. This book does not show the details of hanging arrangements or of inspection/access panels. There are too many ways of accomplishing such things. Use your imagination. You can figure them out. Screws, springs, pegs, hinges, slides, turn-knobs, and keyways can be arranged to do almost any support or access job.

The Construction Plans

If you use "found objects" instead of premium lumber as your birdhouse wood, they're going to be of somewhat different sizes from those shown on the following pages. That doesn't matter. You can juggle the proportions to suit the materials at hand, and to please your own eye for elegance and proportion. Chances are that if you like the illustration on the cover of this book you're already in tune with the design spirit that produced it.

Even after having built more birdhouses than I can count, I still fiddle with the proportions as I go along, sometimes straying considerably from the dimensions I'd worked out earlier. Maybe some aspect of the design needs more emphasis. Maybe the setting demands a longer, shorter, thinner, bolder form. Maybe the height of the viewer's location makes revisions necessary; things look quite different when seen from above (or below) as opposed to straight on. The only thing to remember is that the designs will probably not be helped by a lot of arbitrary changes. They've been pretty thoroughly worked out by trial and error, over the years, to the point that they now seem to be just about as appealing and graceful to most people as they can be, given the physical limitation set by the birds themselves.

Physical Limitations

One of the best-selling books on birdhouse design is called, not surprisingly, The Birdhouse Book. In it, author Don McNeil has gone to great lengths to show in considerable detail many things not shown in this book. He covers, for instance, the exact procedures for laying out, cutting and assembling the pieces needed for his designs. He shows clean-out arrangements, hanging devices, and defenses against predators. He discusses many of the nesting habits and peculiarities of various birds, and he has compiled a table of dimensions that, with his generous permission, I have reproduced below.

Birdhouse and Shelf Dimensions

The following is a summary of important measurements for birdhouses and shelves. There may be variations. For example, tree swallows and violet-green swallows can enter a hole 1¼ inches in diameter instead of 1½ inches (so can the English sparrow). The purple martin of the West has been known to enter a hole 1¾ inches in diameter, instead of 2 inches (so can the starling, according to some authorities). And though a 4-inch entrance is common for wood duck boxes, the one described in this book calls for a 3 by 4-inch entrance, rounded on the horizontal, because it helps to discourage raccoons.

Nor is there a hard-and-fast rule for interior dimensions. These are averages. Birds often accept nest boxes larger or smaller than those listed for the species, as long as they can gain entrance. Perhaps this is due to a shortage of natural nest cavities. With woodpeckers, your chances of success may be improved if you pack the box full of sawdust.

	Birdhouses				
	Entrance Diameter	Entrance above Floor*	Depth of House	Inside of House	Height above Ground
Bewick's wren	1 in.	1 to 6 in.	6 to 8 in.	4 by 4 in.	6 to 10 ft.
House wren	1 in.	1 to 6 in.	6 to 8 in.	4 by 4 in.	6 to 10 ft.
Carolina wren	1⅛ in.	1 to 6 in.	6 to 8 in.	4 by 4 in.	6 to 10 ft.
Chickadee	1⅛ in.	6 to 8 in.	8 to 10 in.	4 by 4 in.	6 to 15 ft.
Downy woodpecker	1¼ in.	6 to 8 in.	8 to 10 in.	4 by 4 in.	6 to 20 ft.
Nuthatch	1¼ in.	6 to 8 in.	8 to 10 in.	4 by 4 in.	12 to 20 ft.
Titmouse	1¼ in.	6 to 8 in.	6 in.	4 by 4 in.	6 to 15 ft.
Tree swallow	1½ in.	1 to 5 in.	6 in.	5 by 5 in.	10 to 15 ft.
Violet-green swallow	1½ in.	1 to 5 in.	6 in.	5 by 5 in.	10 to 15 ft.
Bluebird	1½ in.	6 in.	8 in.	5 by 5 in.	5 to 10 ft.
Hairy woodpecker	2 in.	9 to 12 in.	12 to 15 in.	6 by 6 in.	12 to 20 ft.
Redheaded woodpecker	2 in.	9 to 12 in.	12 to 15 in.	6 by 6 in.	12 to 20 ft.
Golden-fronted	2 in.	9 to 12 in.	16 to 18 in.		10 to 25 ft.

Bird	Diameter of Entrance	Entrance Above Floor*	Depth of House	Inside of House	Height Above Ground
Carolina wren					
Chickadee	1¼ in.	6 to 8 in.	8 to 10 in.	5 by 5 in.	10 to 15 ft.
Downy woodpecker	1¼ in.	6 to 8 in.	6 in.	5 by 5 in.	5 to 10 ft.
Nuthatch	1¼ in.	1 to 5 in.	6 in.	5 by 5 in.	12 to 20 ft.
Titmouse	1½ in.	1 to 5 in.	8 in.	6 by 6 in.	12 to 20 ft.
Tree swallow	1½ in.	6 in.	12 to 15 in.	6 by 6 in.	
Violet-green swallow	1½ in.	9 to 12 in.	12 to 15 in.		12 to 20 ft.
Bluebird	1½ in.	9 to 12 in.		6 by 6 in.	15 to 20 ft.
Hairy woodpecker	2 in.		12 to 15 in.	6 by 6 in.	6 to 20 ft.
Redheaded woodpecker		9 to 12 in.	6 in.	7 by 7 in.	10 to 30 ft.
Golden-fronted woodpecker	2 in.	1 in.	16 to 18 in.	8 by 8 in.	10 to 30 ft.
Purple martin	2 in.	14 to 16 in.	12 to 15 in.	8 by 8 in.	10 to 25 ft.
Flicker	2½ in.	9 to 12 in.	12 to 15 in.	10½ by 10½ in.	12 to 18 ft.
Screech owl	3 in.	9 to 12 in.	24 to 26 in.	15 by 18 in.	
Kestrel (sparrow hawk)	3 in.	18 to 20 in.	15 to 18 in.		
Wood duck	4 in.	4 in.			
Barn owl	6 in.				

*Entrance above floor is measured from the center of the entrance to the floor.

Shelf Nests

Bird	Sides	Depth of House	Inside of House	Height above Ground
Barn swallow	1 or more sides open	6 in.	6 by 6 in.	8 to 12 ft.
Phoebe	1 or more sides open	6 in.	6 by 6 in.	8 to 12 ft.
Robin	1 or more sides open	8 in.	8 by 8 in.	6 to 15 ft.
Song sparrow	All sides open	6 in.	6 by 6 in.	1 to 3 ft.

You can see that many of my designs do not conform to the McNeil criteria. Too often, I'm afraid, I let architectural considerations outweigh what might be called the engineering criteria of birdhouse design . . . and still the birds used my houses! Whether that was the result of desperation on their part, or some unexpected flexibility in the birds' special needs, I can't say but I feel sure that when and if you stray from my designs you should stray in the direction of the table above.

A Final Word

Get out there and build something beautiful!

— Malcolm Wells, Architect
   Brewster, Cape Cod
   Massachusetts
   Late in the Twentieth Century

Architect's Sketchbook

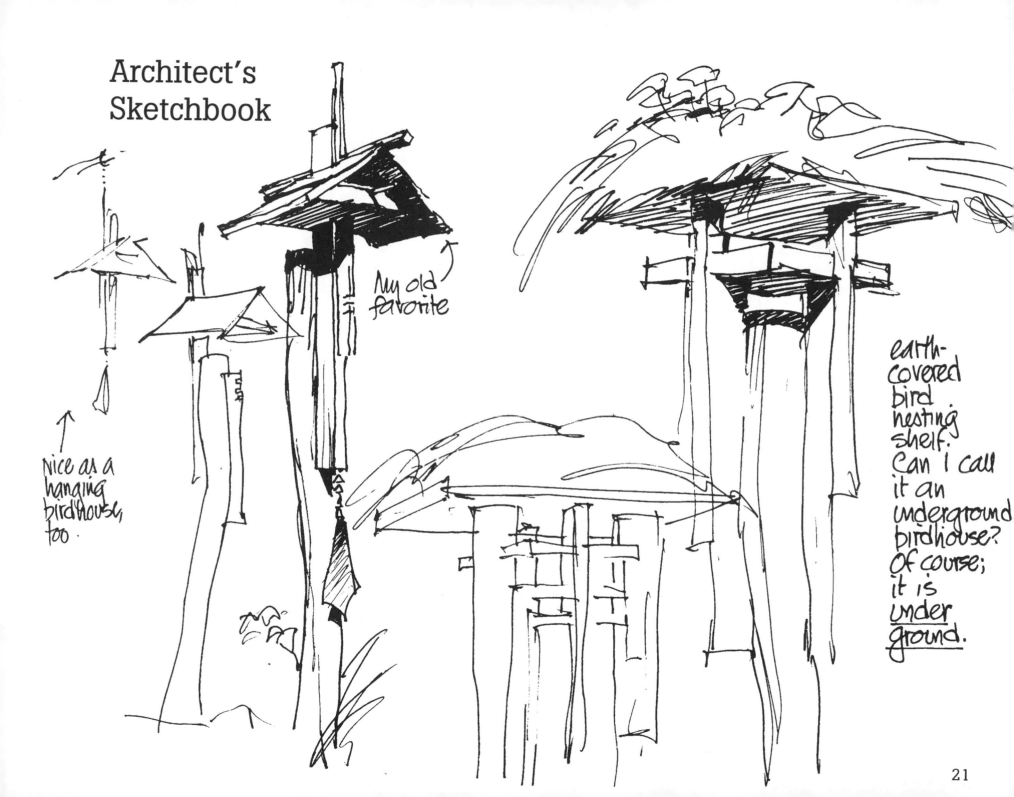

My old favorite

nice as a hanging birdhouse, too.

earth-covered bird nesting shelf. Can I call it an underground birdhouse? Of course; it is <u>under</u> <u>ground</u>.

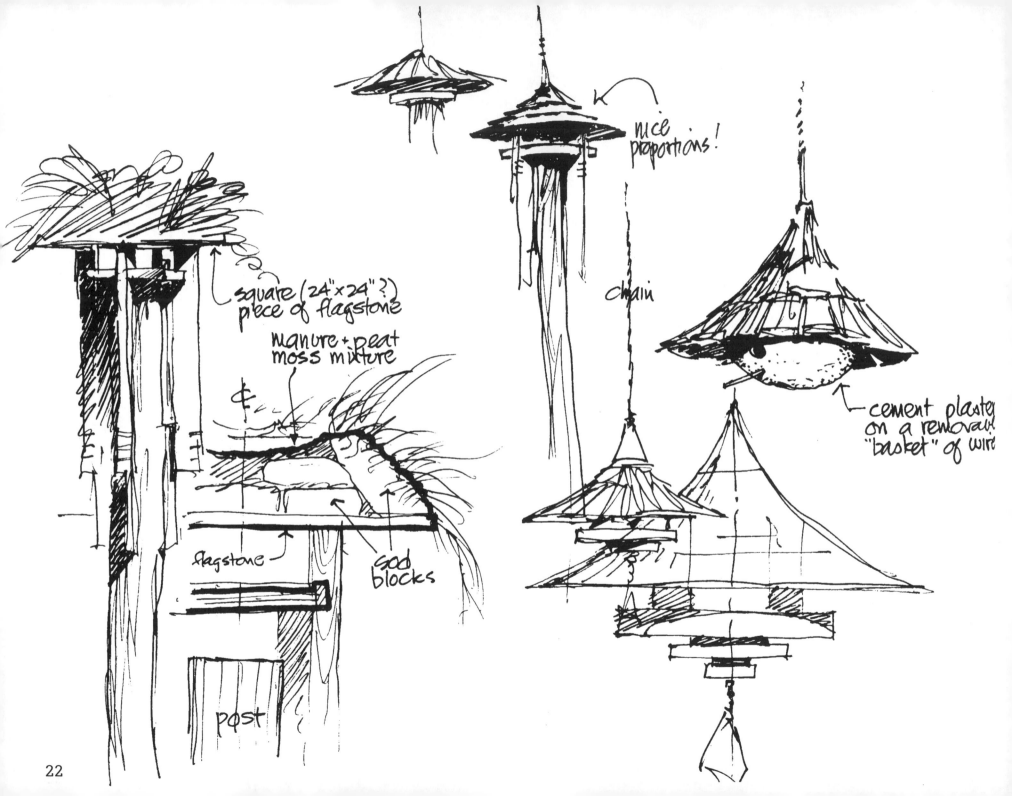

square (24"x24"?)
piece of flagstone

manure + peat
moss mixture

nice
proportions!

chain

cement plaster
on a removable
"basket" of wire

flagstone

sod
blocks

post

22

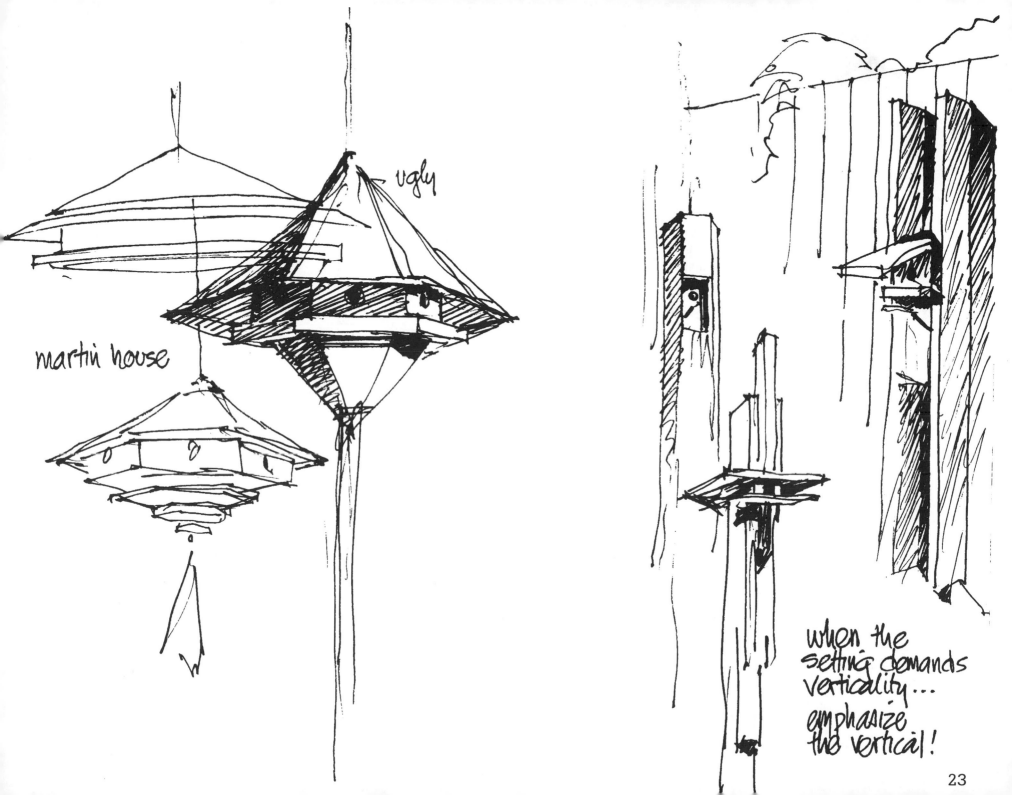

ugly

martin house

when the
setting demands
verticality...
emphasize
the vertical!

23

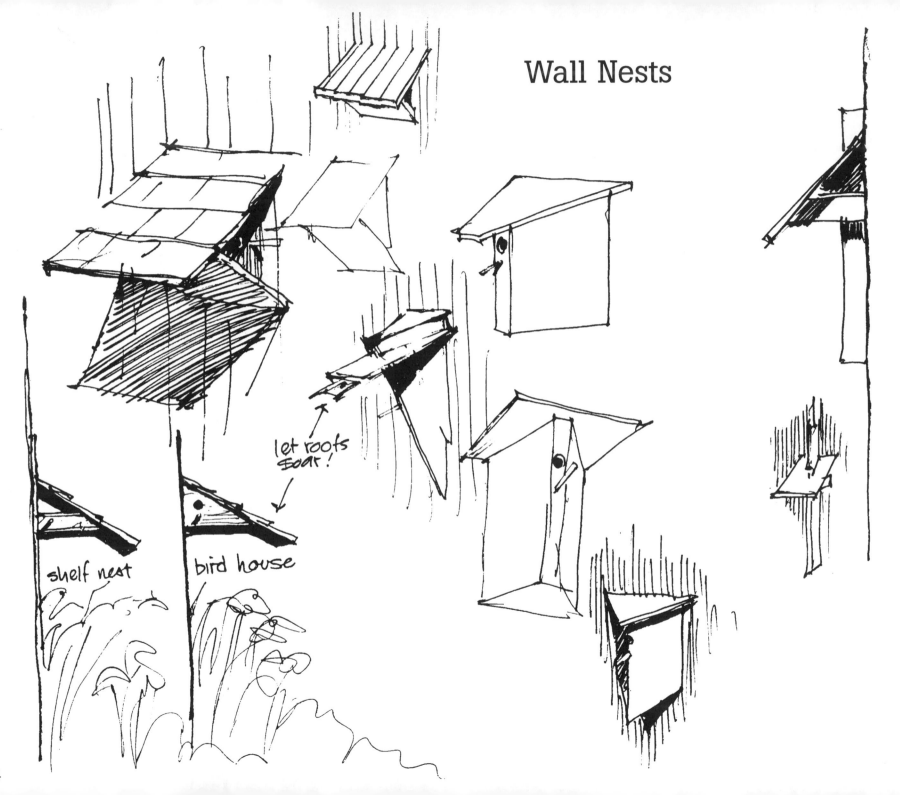

Wall Nests

let roofs soar!

shelf nest

bird house

24

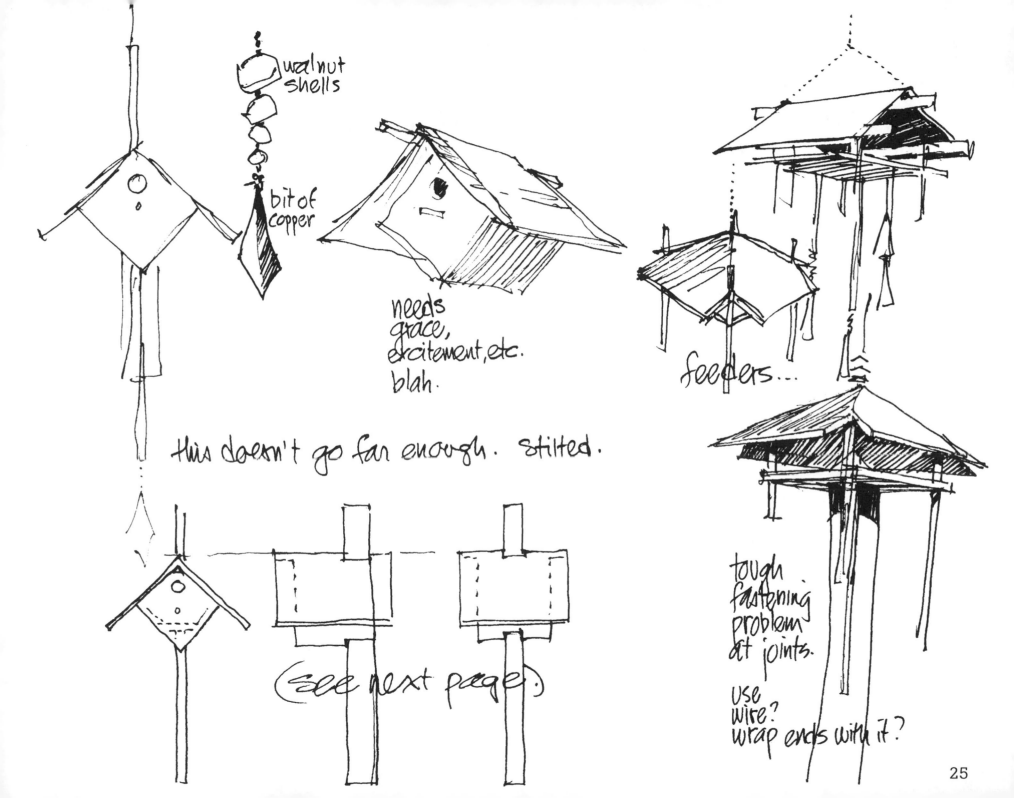

walnut shells

bit of copper

needs grace, excitement, etc. blah.

this doesn't go far enough. stilted.

(see next page)

feeders...

tough fastening problem at joints.

use wire? wrap ends with it?

25

The trouble with this design  is that it fights its own geometry. First of all, the hole should be this shape: ◆. Second, the implied vertical of the centerline brings in a conflicting system. This birdhouse has to say 45 degrees with all its heart.

Now we're talking!

add little perches all over the place but maintain the 45 degrees!

ideal on diagonal lattice...

...or on an old wistaria-covered post.

(don't pass the 2x3 through the post; add a little fake tail.) Just keep the geometry going.

But don't get the idea that any of this matters to the wrens. I hope it does but I have nothing to confirm my hope. They're probably happy with the old basic cube, 4" on a side, no matter how mindless it seems to us. What matters is that we try to do what they do so well when left alone.

And what about a squirrel-proof, hanging bird feeder? Try this. The projecting wires are straightened sections of your husband's coat hangers, held (with screws) to the edge of the roof. A long threaded rod goes up through the center of the whole thing.

A circular version with a conical metal roof would be easy, too.

ventilated
double roof

← p.19 is better.

Some vertical designs
for use where the up-and-down
emphasis is strong,
(as in a wooded area).

And this might be appealing,
too, especially if the nest-
space were recessed into the post
(see dotted line).

But wait a minute: why go to all this trouble just for a birdhouse?
Because now that we know there's something better than this:
we have no choice.

It's a good place to start
but then let it develop.
More roof shelter, then stronger verticals.
Soon they'll want to grow by themselves.
Let the design be all that it wants to be.
I mean, you got the lumber for nothing,
so why not? You'll be greatly rewarded.

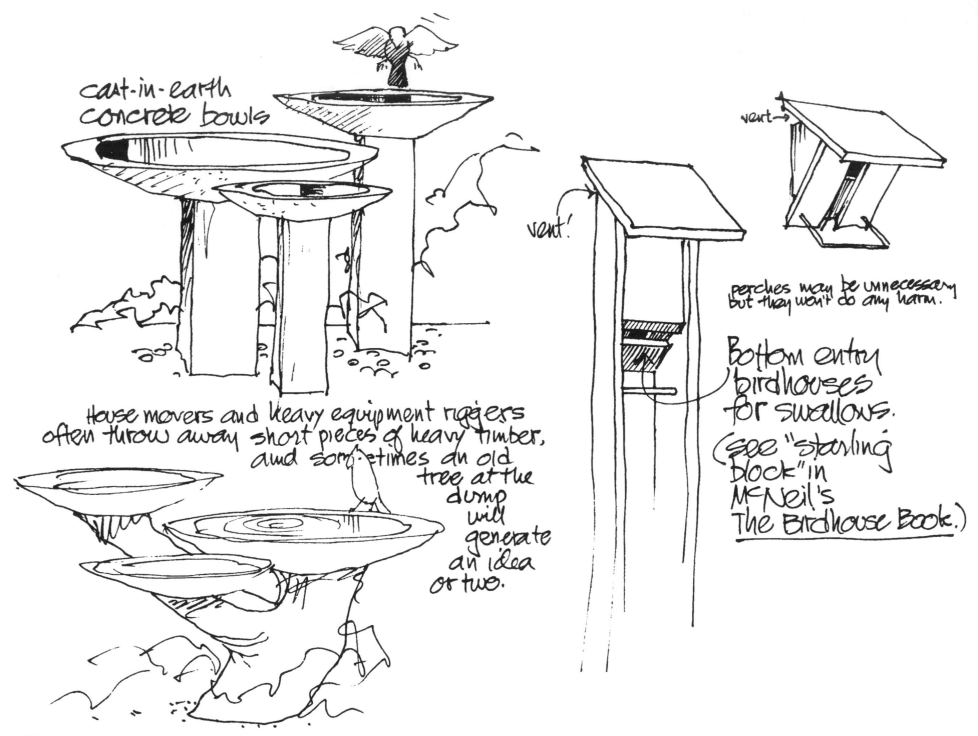

cast-in-earth concrete bowls

House movers and heavy equipment riggers often throw away short pieces of heavy timber, and sometimes an old tree at the dump will generate an idea or two.

vent!

vent →

perches may be unnecessary but they won't do any harm.

Bottom entry birdhouses for swallows.
(see "starling block" in McNeil's The Birdhouse Book.)

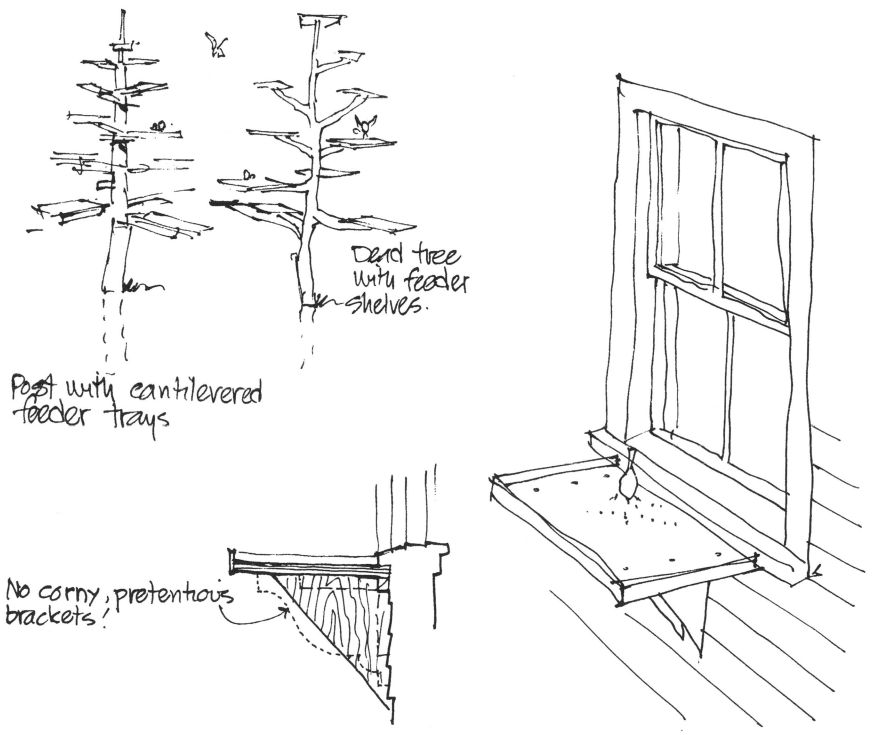

Post with cantilevered
feeder trays

Dead tree
with feeder
shelves.

No corny, pretentious
brackets!

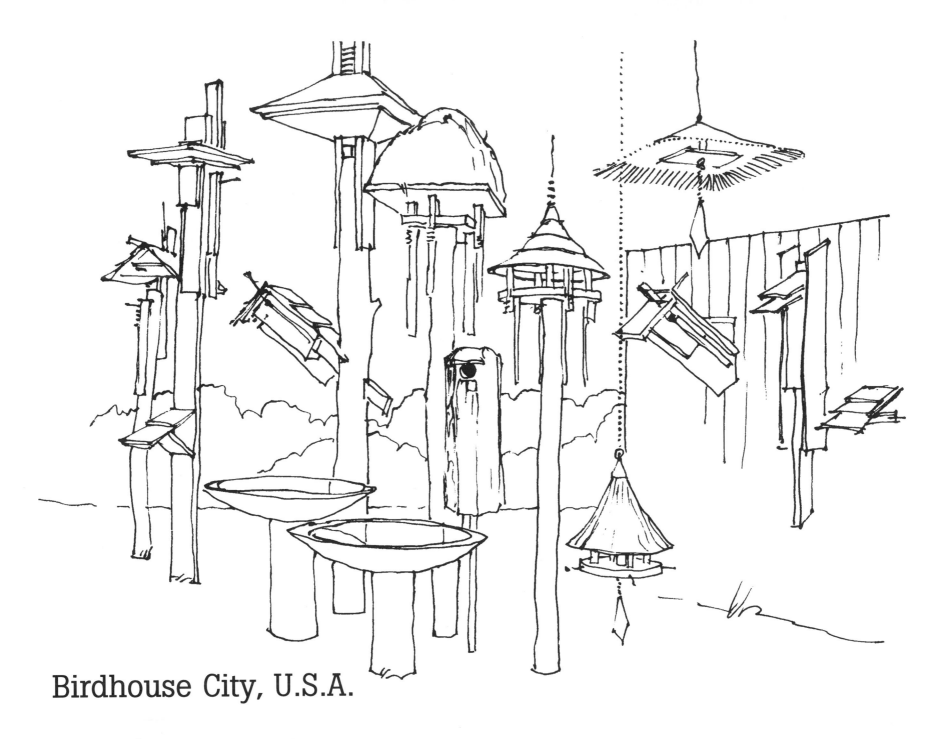

Birdhouse City, U.S.A.

Construction Plans

Safety

This wouldn't be a bad place for a word about care while working with tools, so be careful down there in the basement! if you get blood on the birdhouse you could drive away the very creatures you hope to attract. Besides, bloodstains are unsightly, and they could mean that you've been seriously hurt.

Remember to do what the warnings printed with the tool instructions tell you to do. Then the whole birdhouse experience can be a pleasant one.

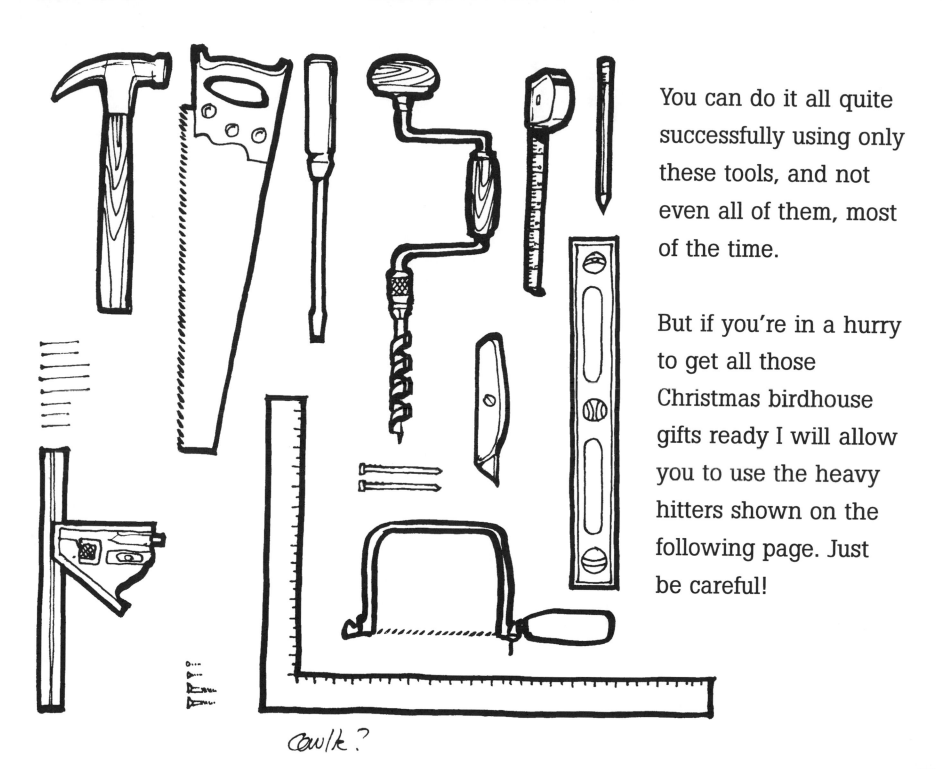

You can do it all quite successfully using only these tools, and not even all of them, most of the time.

But if you're in a hurry to get all those Christmas birdhouse gifts ready I will allow you to use the heavy hitters shown on the following page. Just be careful!

caulk?

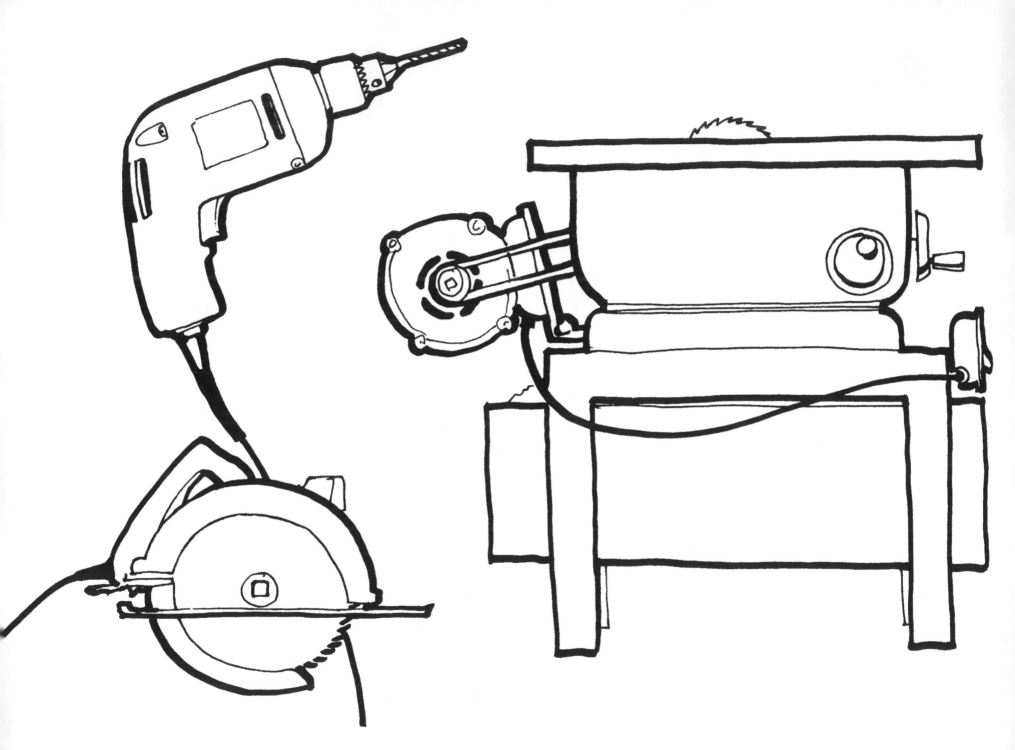

H1
My Old Favorite

Designed primarily for shelf-nesters (barn swallows, robins, phoebes, and song sparrows) this house has been occupied by many other birds as well. Last summer, a pair of catbirds hung around for days considering a summer lease but then decided it wasn't quite their kind of house.

The cover illustration is a good description of this house but perhaps this parts list would be helpful . . .

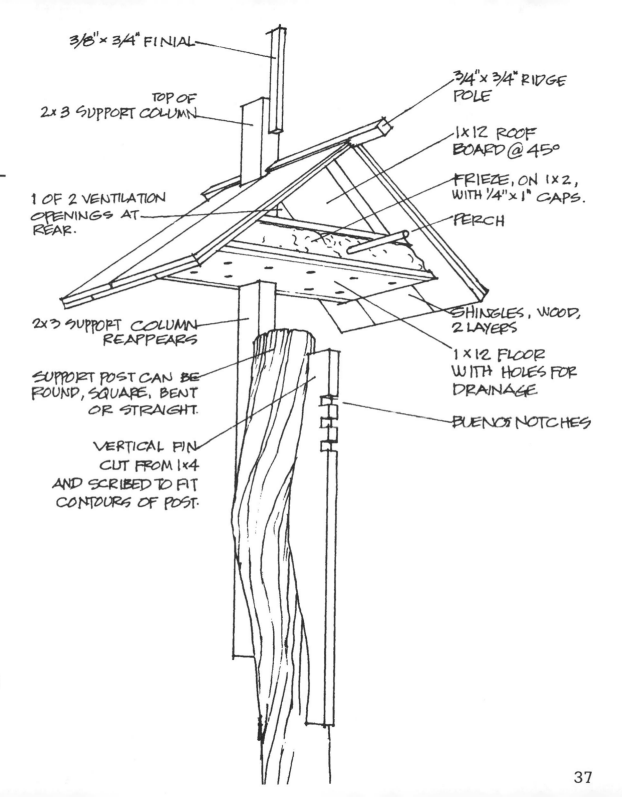

3/8" x 3/4" FINIAL

TOP OF
2 x 3 SUPPORT COLUMN

3/4" x 3/4" RIDGE POLE

1 x 12 ROOF BOARD @ 45°

FRIEZE, ON 1 x 2, WITH 1/4" x 1" CAPS.

PERCH

1 OF 2 VENTILATION OPENINGS AT REAR.

2 x 3 SUPPORT COLUMN REAPPEARS

SHINGLES, WOOD, 2 LAYERS

1 x 12 FLOOR WITH HOLES FOR DRAINAGE

BUENO! NOTCHES

SUPPORT POST CAN BE ROUND, SQUARE, BENT OR STRAIGHT.

VERTICAL FIN CUT FROM 1 x 4 AND SCRIBED TO FIT CONTOURS OF POST.

These two drawings are at 3/8" scale (3/8" equals one inch). The actual birdhouse is almost three times as large. After you read the notes, the construction should be easy to understand but if it's not, turn the page to see an explanatory diagram.

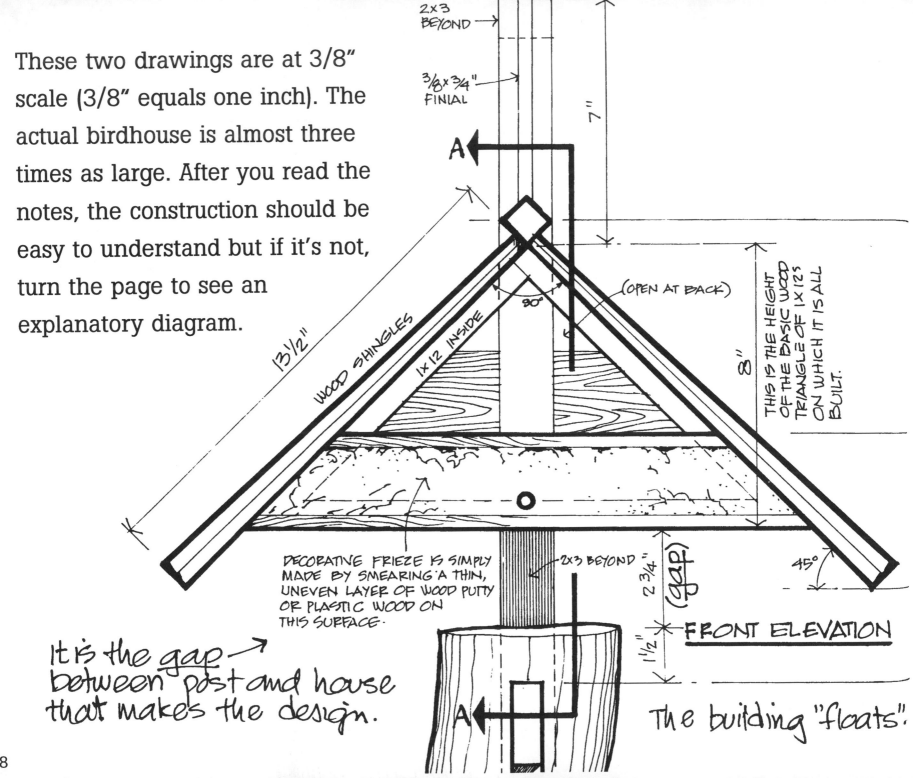

2x3 BEYOND

3/8 x 3/4" FINIAL

7"

A

13 1/2"

WOOD SHINGLES

1x12 INSIDE

30°

(OPEN AT BACK)

THIS IS THE HEIGHT OF THE BASIC WOOD TRIANGLE OF 1x12'S ON WHICH IT IS ALL BUILT.

8"

DECORATIVE FRIEZE IS SIMPLY MADE BY SMEARING A THIN, UNEVEN LAYER OF WOOD PUTTY OR PLASTIC WOOD ON THIS SURFACE.

2x3 BEYOND

2 3/4" (gap)

1 1/2"

45°

FRONT ELEVATION

It is the gap → between post and house that makes the design.

A

The building "floats".

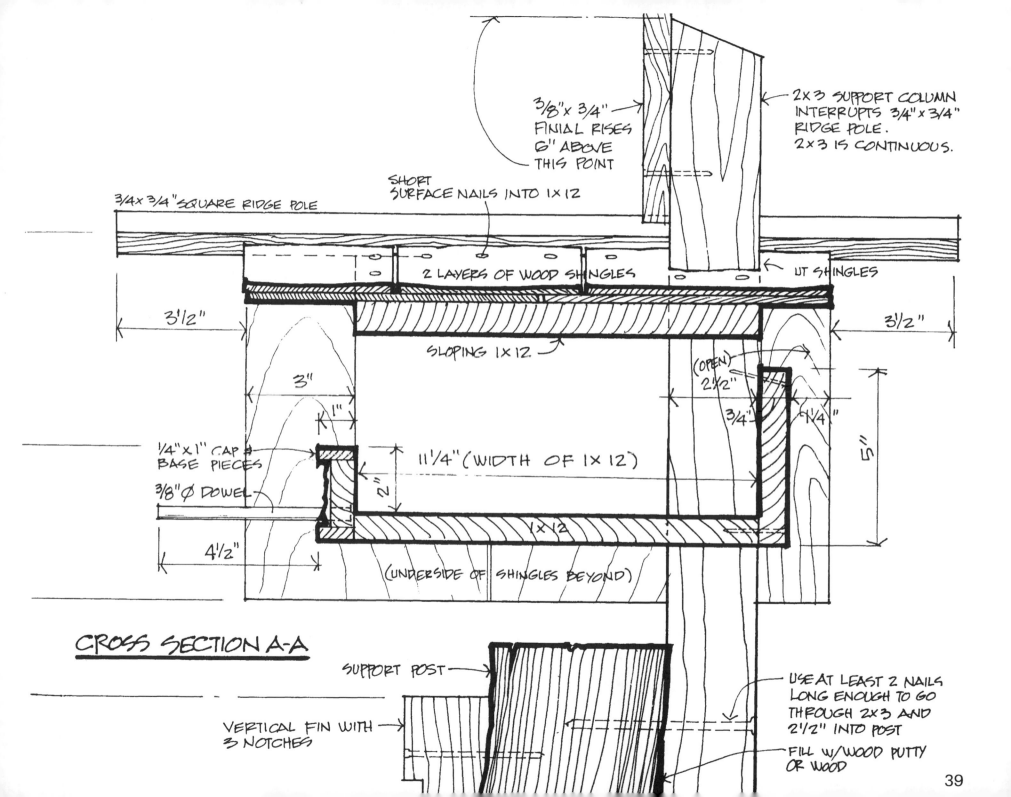

3/8" x 3/4" FINIAL RISES 6" ABOVE THIS POINT

2x3 SUPPORT COLUMN INTERRUPTS 3/4" x 3/4" RIDGE POLE. 2x3 IS CONTINUOUS.

3/4 x 3/4" SQUARE RIDGE POLE

SHORT SURFACE NAILS INTO 1x12

2 LAYERS OF WOOD SHINGLES

UT SHINGLES

3'1/2"

3 1/2"

SLOPING 1x12

3"

(OPEN) 2 1/2"

3/4"

1/4"

1"

5"

1/4" x 1" CAP & BASE PIECES

11 1/4" (WIDTH OF 1x12)

2"

3/8" Ø DOWEL

1x12

4 1/2"

(UNDERSIDE OF SHINGLES BEYOND)

CROSS SECTION A-A

SUPPORT POST

VERTICAL FIN WITH 3 NOTCHES

USE AT LEAST 2 NAILS LONG ENOUGH TO GO THROUGH 2x3 AND 2 1/2" INTO POST

FILL w/ WOOD PUTTY OR WOOD

39

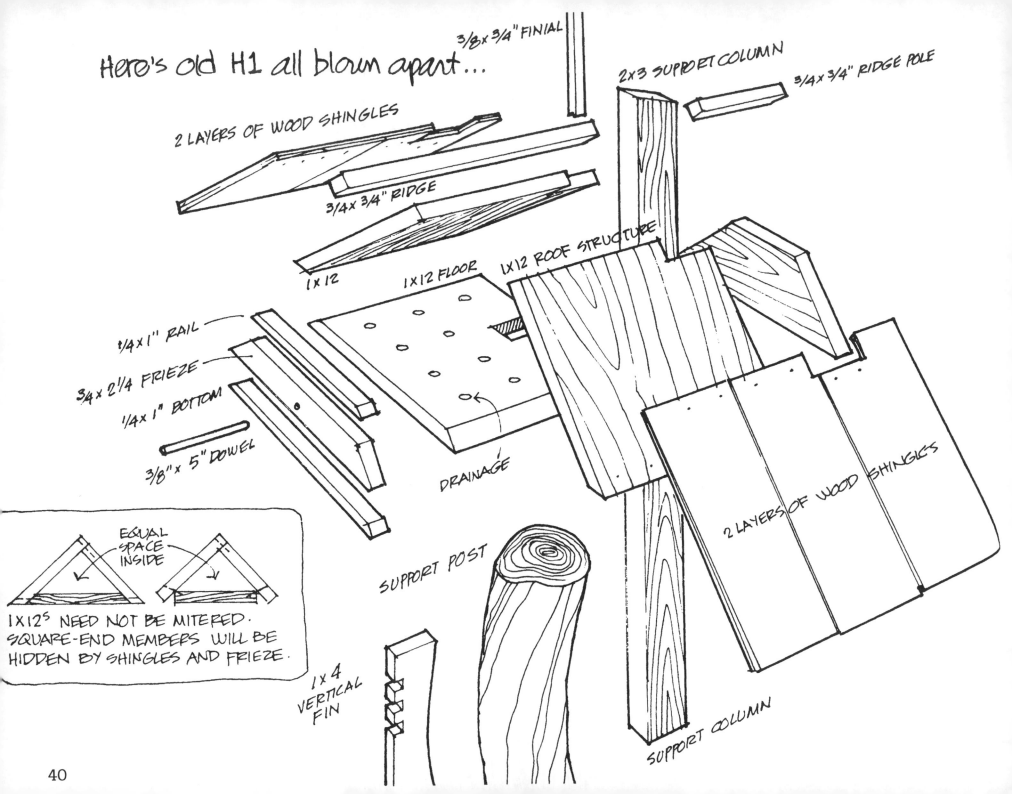

Here's old H1 all blown apart...

3/8 x 3/4" FINIAL

2 x 3 SUPPORT COLUMN

3/4 x 3/4" RIDGE POLE

2 LAYERS OF WOOD SHINGLES

3/4 x 3/4" RIDGE

1 x 12

1 x 12 FLOOR

1 x 12 ROOF STRUCTURE

1/4 x 1" RAIL

3/4 x 2 1/4 FRIEZE

1/4 x 1" BOTTOM

3/8" x 5" DOWEL

DRAINAGE

2 LAYERS OF WOOD SHINGLES

EQUAL SPACE INSIDE

1 X 12'S NEED NOT BE MITERED. SQUARE-END MEMBERS WILL BE HIDDEN BY SHINGLES AND FRIEZE.

SUPPORT POST

1 x 4 VERTICAL FIN

SUPPORT COLUMN

40

I've always thought that a hanging version of H1 would be appealing, too. Birds seem not to mind it at all if their house sways in the breeze. They evolved in swaying houses.

All you have to remember when converting this, or any of the designs, from post-supported to suspended are:

1) be sure the hanger chain, wire, or rope is rugged enough not to cause any sudden letdowns, and
2) locate the suspension so that the house doesn't hang crookedly. In birdhouse architecture as in human architecture, plumbness (true verticality) is important. If you were designing a suspended human abode you'd have to find, using math, its center of gravity in order to avoid great embarrassment at the building site, but when you're dealing with birdhouses trial and error, at the moment of hanging them, will locate the point from which the structure must be hung.

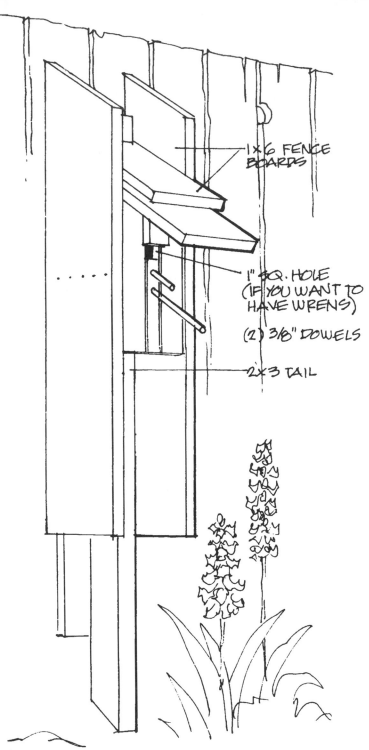

1×6 FENCE BOARDS

1" SQ. HOLE (IF YOU WANT TO HAVE WRENS)

(2) 3/8" DOWELS

2×3 TAIL

H2
"The Fence Board House"

Camouflage is not limited to trickery with color. Line and form are part of it, too. Here, on a vertical-board fence, we mounted a vertical-board house. It fitted in so perfectly it seemed to have grown there.

Its secondary theme — the 30° angle — was dictated by the need for a water-shedding roof, which led to the double-layered ventilating idea. The house front comes off for inspection and clean-out, revealing a floor much higher than you'd guess. It's up where that line of nail heads is exposed. I thought the square hole would attract a square wren but, so far, all we've seen have been the conventional round ones.

Here are the dimensions. On the next page you'll find the construction details.

Remember that the proportions and dimensions can be changed to better suit the background, the materials available, and the eye of the birdhouse builder.

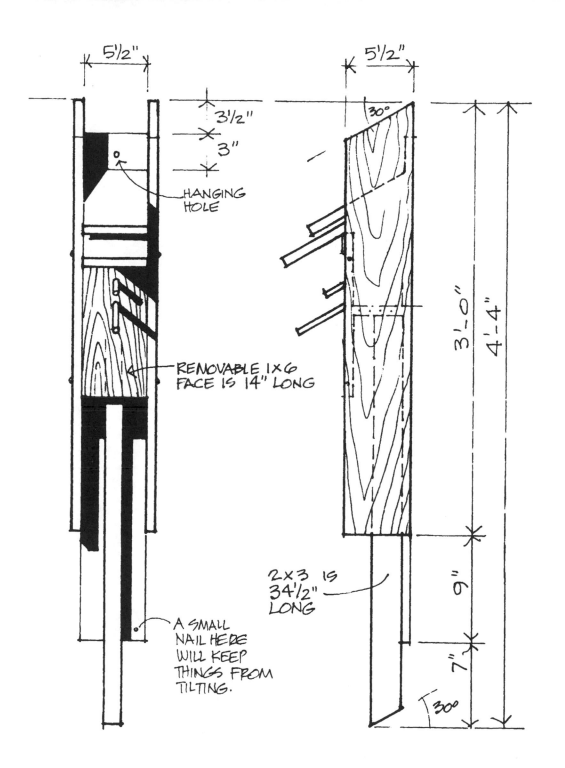

5½"

3½"

3"

HANGING HOLE

REMOVABLE 1X6 FACE IS 14" LONG

A SMALL NAIL HERE WILL KEEP THINGS FROM TILTING.

5½"

30°

3'-0"

4'-4"

2X3 IS 34½" LONG

9"

7"

30°

Here it is: the world's first peek inside the vertical-boarded, roof-ventilated birdhouse. No wonder the wrens love it so. What could be more appealing? Tastefully simple in design, and well-drained as well as cool in summer, "The Fence Board House" seems to have it all.

And if creating those 30° slopes is a problem, just pick any slope of about that amount and make sure all the angled parts follow it. It's the consistency that matters.

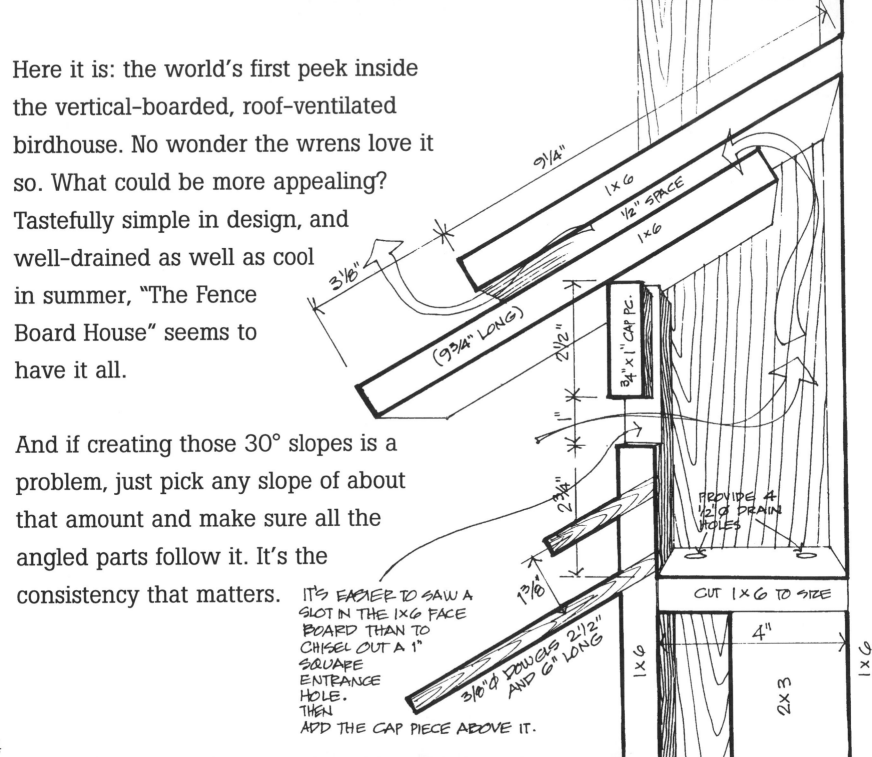

9¼"

1 x 6

½" SPACE

1 x 6

3⅛"

(9¾" LONG)

2½"

¾" x 1" CAP PC.

1"

2¾"

PROVIDE 4
½" ∅ DRAIN
HOLES

1⅜"

CUT 1 x 6 TO SIZE

4"

1 x 6

2 x 3

1 x 6

IT'S EASIER TO SAW A
SLOT IN THE 1 X 6 FACE
BOARD THAN TO
CHISEL OUT A 1"
SQUARE
ENTRANCE
HOLE.
THEN
ADD THE CAP PIECE ABOVE IT.

3/8" ∅ DOWELS 2½"
AND 6" LONG

Poles and Posts

It's tempting to think of using a nice straight post made of treated lumber when you plan a birdhouse-on-a-pole but that stuff is bad news. If carpenters are warned not to breathe its sawdust think what it must do to all the bugs and worms and spiders — not to mention birds — in its vicinity. Far better, it seems, to use untreated wood, the more natural the better. In the woods you can find plenty of dead branches that will do the job. And if they happen to be locust or some other

CUT LINE

SCRIBING A BOARD TO FIT A CURVED POST.

slow-to-rot wood, so much the better. Posts can be replaced every few years without much trouble.

It is a law of nature that birdhouses,
particularly those on poles, will always
become 293% heavier when
it's time to erect them.

You can do it, though, and we're all counting on you.

Make sure it's vertical.—

The dirt never fits back into the hole but you can get most of it in, even with a post filling some of the space, by tamping the soil in about 6" layers as you replace the earth. The business end of the tamper should be small — 1-1/2 to 2" across. That's why the long handle of a long-handled shovel works so well. If the tamper-end gets much larger you might as well use your foot, which is too big to do a thorough job. If the earth isn't solidly packed, or if the hole isn't deep enough, wind will sway the structure, loosening the earth around its base.

How deep should the hole be? It depends on the type of soil, the height of the post, the diameter of the post, and how many Wheaties you ate for breakfast. A general rule, however, for posts in the 8-to-12 foot range, is from 2 feet to 2-1/2 feet. You can tell, by testing the post, how rigid it is, and after a few installations you'll know, intuitively, how deep to dig.

H3
The Wood Duck* Nest Box

Architecturally, this may be the toughest job of all. Mounting a vertical solid on a sloping tree trunk — or on a metal post hammered into pond-bottom muck — means a design conflict. The best approach seems to be simplicity and rusticity, and forget trying to blend into the background. It's best to begin by checking to see if wood ducks live in your area. If they do, head for water. Their nests should be over or near water. Square tall boxes are commonly used but an octagonal shape is easy to build and it will look less out of place, particularly when you cover it with slabs of bark or decayed wood.

Wood ducks bring no nesting materials to the birdhouse, so you have to put 4" of sawdust or planer shavings in the bottom.

* wood duck.

But there are other kinds as well ... live ones that nest in birdhouses.

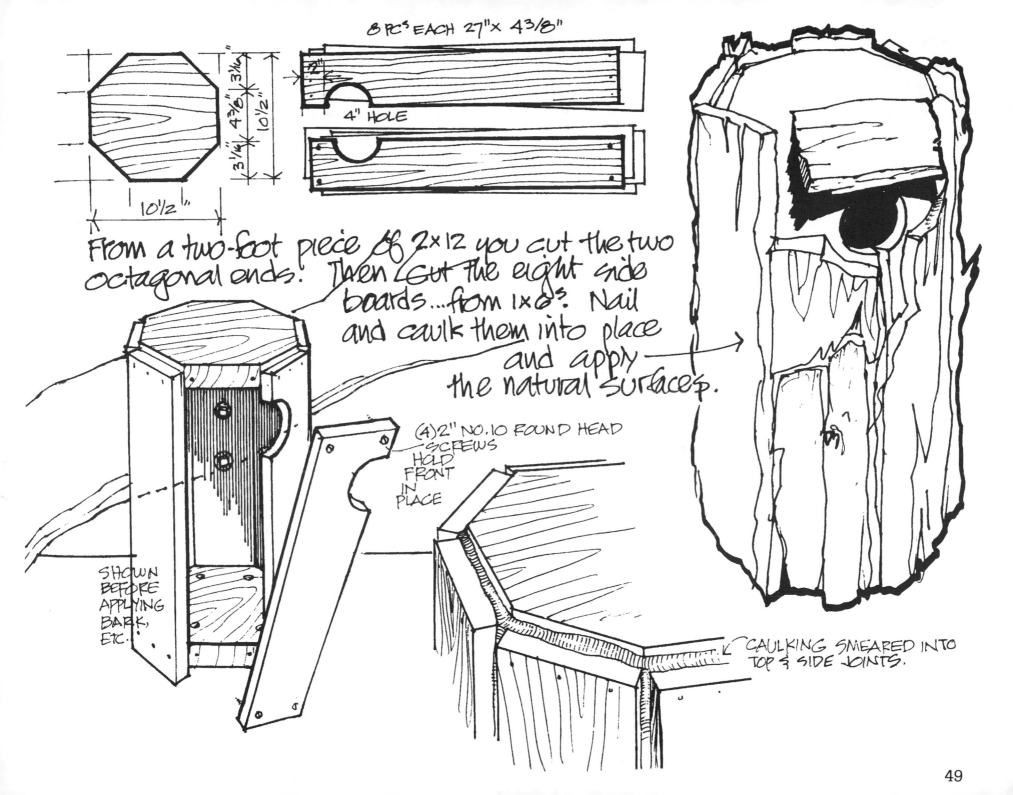

8 PCS EACH 27" x 4 3/8"

4" HOLE

10 1/2"

10 1/2"

4 3/8" 3 3/16"

3 3/16"

From a two-foot piece of 2×12 you cut the two octagonal ends. Then cut the eight side boards...from 1×6s. Nail and caulk them into place and apply the natural surfaces.

SHOWN BEFORE APPLYING BARK, ETC.

(4) 2" NO.10 ROUND HEAD SCREWS HOLD FRONT IN PLACE

CAULKING SMEARED INTO TOP & SIDE JOINTS.

49

Lag screws, or lag bolts, are needed to hold this nest securely to a tree.

SMALL WOOD SHIM

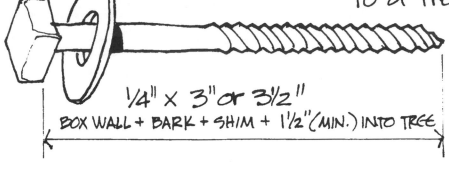

1/4" × 3" or 3½"
BOX WALL + BARK + SHIM + 1½"(MIN.) INTO TREE

4" OF SAWDUST OR PLANER CHIPS

NOTE UP-SLOPING ½" HOLES FOR VENTILATION.

height: 6 or 8 feet above water, 10 to 20 feet above the ground when mounting on a tree.

I've used a caulking material called Pheno-seal with great success. It sticks to almost every material, can be finger-smeared into place, and it comes in a brown color that tends to disappear among natural materials. A little rainwater won't kill a duck but the interior of this nest box might as well be dry and comfortable, at least as dry and comfortable as its natural counterpart, a hollow tree. It must be at least as easy to climb out out of, too. That's why you see the "ladder" of expanded metal tacked up the inside wall, to the entrance hole, on the cross section at left. The ducklings need a way to get up there, and boards, even rough ones, don't offer the grips they need.

Here's the way you mount the nest box over water when no fallen tree or low branch is available.

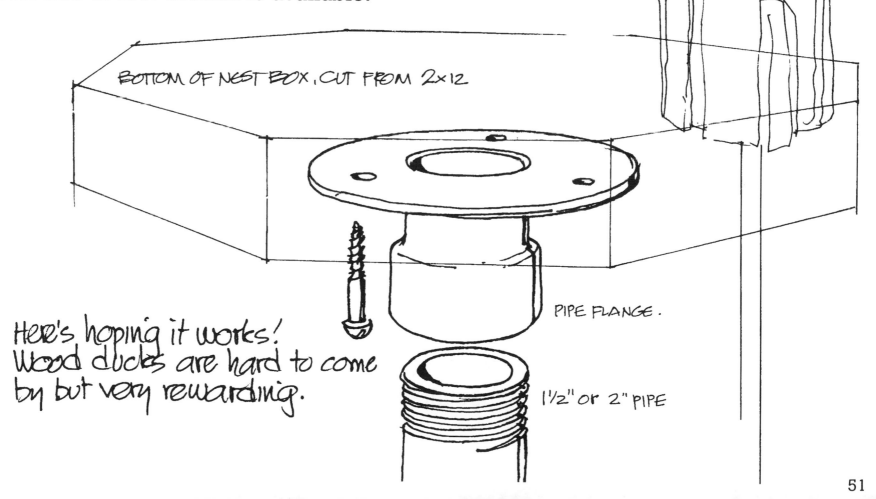

BOTTOM OF NEST BOX, CUT FROM 2×12

Here's hoping it works! Wood ducks are hard to come by but very rewarding.

PIPE FLANGE.

1½" or 2" PIPE

H4
The Underground Birdhouse

When I first decided to design an underground birdhouse I thought, naturally, of a conventional one set beneath the ground. But then someone pointed out to me the fact that birds are more sky oriented than earthbound. When I accepted that revelation, the current underground design began to take form in my imagination. I saw it as a high nesting shelf protected by a widely overhanging mass of wildflowers . . . a roof shape having this sort of contour: But after testing such an arrangement during the great summer drought of '88, I soon discovered that only a great high mound of water-holding mulch would keep the plants alive and the birds comfortable. I'd planned, of course, to find the old reliable open-shelf nesters — robins and their cousins — moving in but to my surprise the shady platform was almost immediately taken over by purple finches, which are red. They said they'd never before had such an enjoyable time on Cape Cod.

Obviously, the success of the design is based on its water-holding capacity, and that capacity is based on natural principles we've only now begun to rediscover as we move into the era of limited water supplies. Mulch, topsoil, compost, roots, shade, and a reservoir combine to carry the process along from rainstorm to rainstorm.

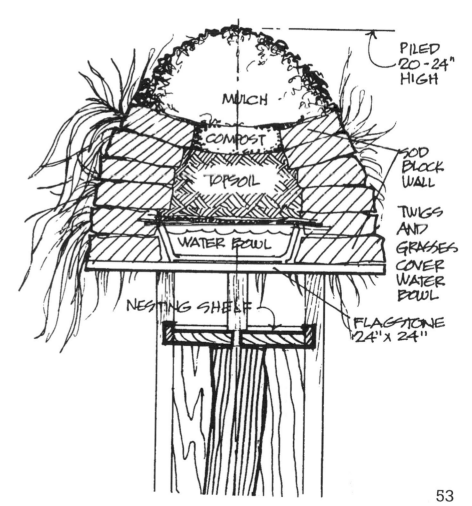

PILED 20-24" HIGH

MULCH

COMPOST

TOPSOIL

SOD BLOCK WALL

TWIGS AND GRASSES COVER WATER BOWL

WATER BOWL

NESTING SHELF

FLAGSTONE 24" x 24"

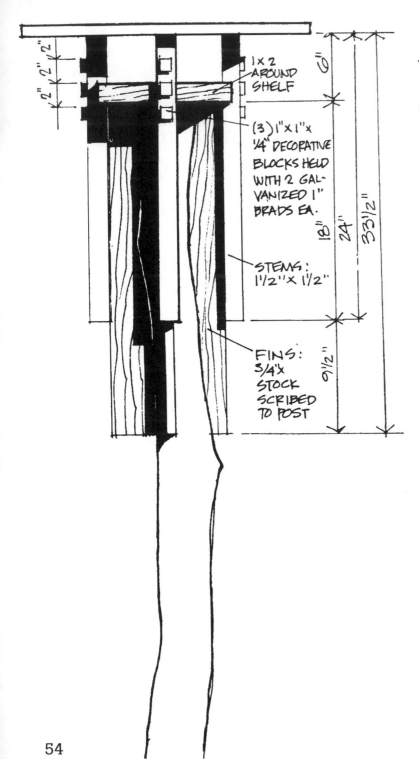

1 x 2 AROUND SHELF

(3) 1"x1"x 1/4" DECORATIVE BLOCKS HELD WITH 2 GALVANIZED 1" BRADS EA.

STEMS: 1 1/2"x 1 1/2"

FINS: 3/4"x STOCK SCRIBED TO POST

6"

18"

24"

33 1/2"

9 1/2"

2" 2" 2" 2"

When the first birdhouse of this design went up on Cape Cod the local papers ran pictures of it as the world's first underground birdhouse. I was delighted by the publicity not because it would help sell books but because we need so desperately to put most of our ugliness underground. Farms and forests all around the world are giving way to asphalt, concrete, and the most wasteful kinds of buildings. If we buried our shopping centers and our parking lots, our factories and our offices we'd have the beautiful green out-of-doors all around us again. And if we buried our houses, and did it the right way, they'd be sunny, dry, energy efficient, easy to maintain, permanent and safe.

That's why aging architects design earth covered bird-houses. It isn't that the birds don't appreciate them. They do. But the priority lies with architecture for humans.

When you see what a pleasant healthy wild garden this can be it won't take a great flight of the imagination to see in your mind's eye the world of the future, in which windows in the hillsides will be the only clue that a city is near.

So get out there and build. You'll be doing both the birds and yourself a big favor.

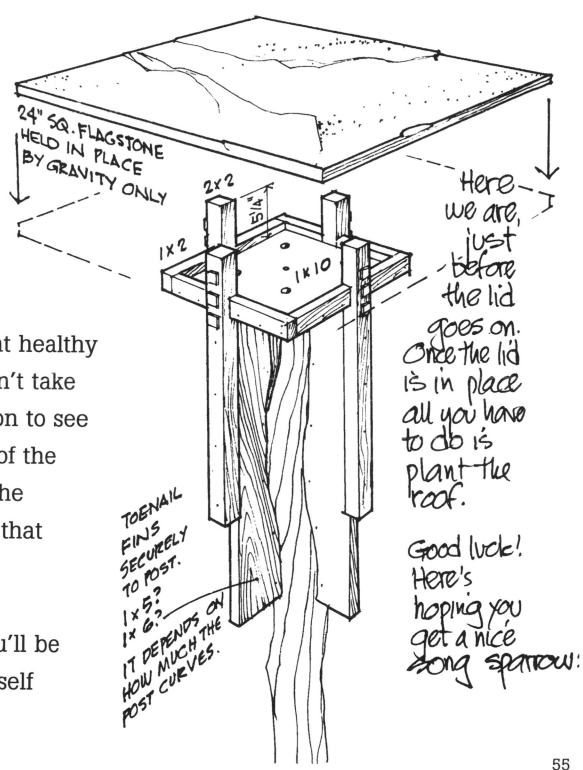

24" SQ. FLAGSTONE HELD IN PLACE BY GRAVITY ONLY

2x2

1x2

5¼"

1x10

TOENAIL FINS SECURELY TO POST. 1x5? 1x6? IT DEPENDS ON HOW MUCH THE POST CURVES.

Here we are, just before the lid goes on. Once the lid is in place all you have to do is plant the roof.

Good luck! Here's hoping you get a nice song sparrow!

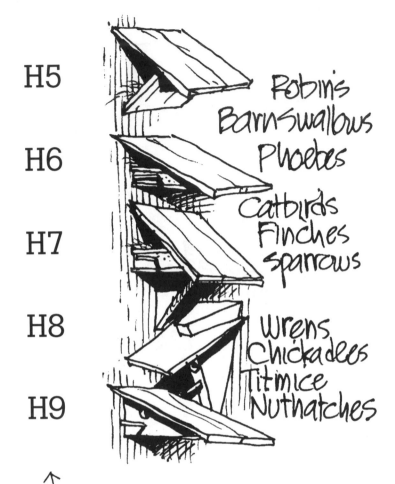

H5 — Robins
Barnswallows
H6 — Phoebes
Catbirds
H7 — Finches
Sparrows
H8 — Wrens
Chickadees
H9 — Titmice
Nuthatches

(Have you gathered by now that "H" stands for house? If you have, you must suspect that after the H's will come some F's)

The Five Wallhouses

The construction and mounting of these houses are so similar it seems best to introduce them together, and then, as their details are developed, to let their differences appear.

The sketches at left show at a glance the general designs of the five birdhouses but they don't show the two most important elements of each: their natural settings, and fitting to the wall.

H5
The Coop

I cannot stress too much the need for at least partial concealment. The nesting birds must be able to see out but we need not see in. Birdhouses are intended to attract birds to a natural setting, not replace it. And a half-hidden birdhouse is much more attractive to human eyes as well. Any naturalist or well-informed nurseryman can tell you the names of shrubs, trees and vines that are native to your area and will provide food for the birds.

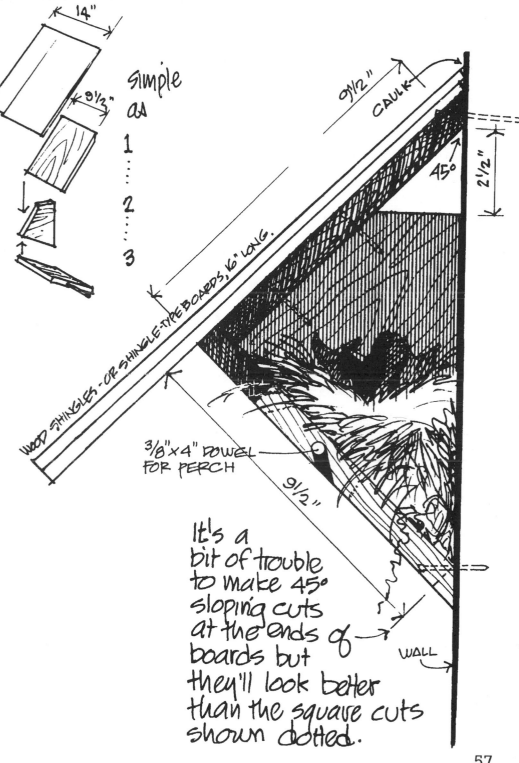

simple as

1 ....
2 ....
3

14"

9½"

WOOD SHINGLES - OR SHINGLE-TYPE BOARDS, 16" LONG.

9½"

CAULK

45°

2½"

3/8"x4" DOWEL FOR PERCH

9½"

It's a bit of trouble to make 45° sloping cuts at the ends of boards but they'll look better than the square cuts shown dotted.

WALL

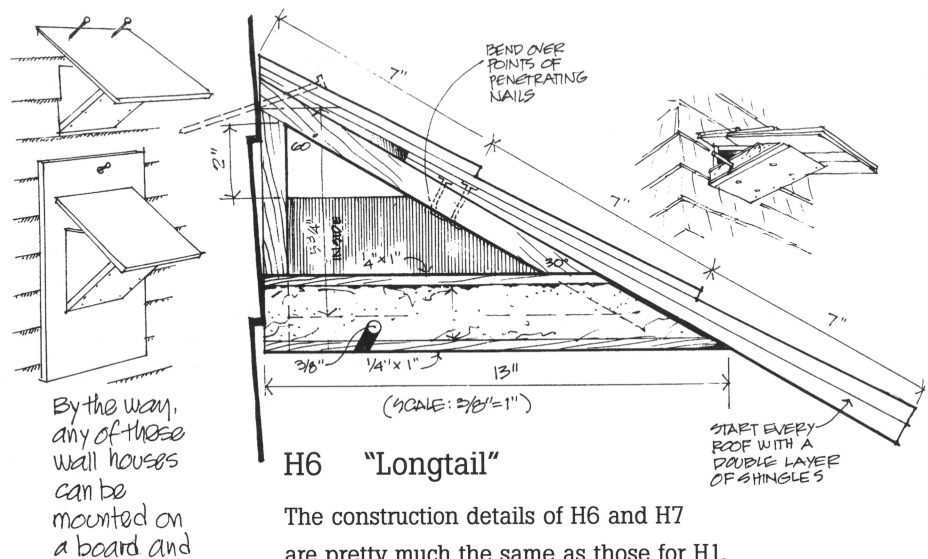

BEND OVER POINTS OF PENETRATING NAILS

7"

2"

60°

7"

5¾"

4"x1"

30°

3/8"

¼"x1"

13"

7"

(SCALE: 3/8"=1")

START EVERY ROOF WITH A DOUBLE LAYER OF SHINGLES

By the way, any of these wall houses can be mounted on a board and hung on a nail instead of directly to the wall.

H6   "Longtail"

The construction details of H6 and H7
are pretty much the same as those for H1,
so little more need be said except for a reminder that
scribing (cutting the back wall of the birdhouse to fit
the shingles or siding of the wall) is desirable.

→

Seen from above — from a second floor window, for instance — not much activity will be apparent at this birdhouse. It's much more interesting observed from below. But if a location below a second floor seems best, let that be the deciding factor. The birds come first. Using the mounting-height table on Page 14, select the ideal location and go on to your next project. Still a lot of birdhouses to build.

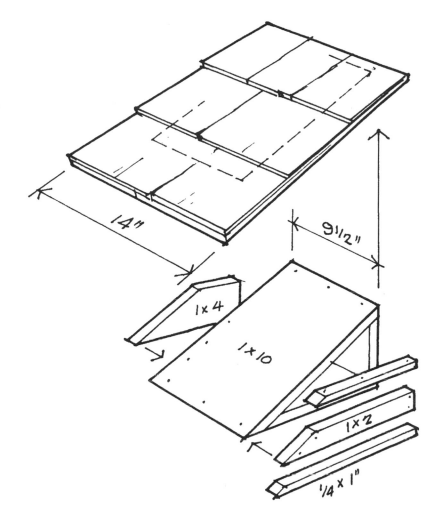

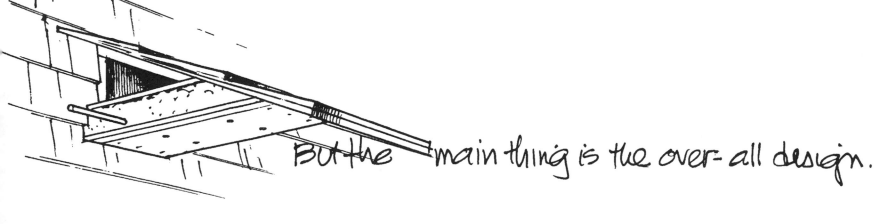

But the main thing is the over-all design.

H7
The Bracket House

Take the birdhouse on the cover, cut it in half, change the proportions a bit, and you have the Bracket House plenty big enough for robins as well as all their fellow shelf-nesters. This birdhouse will have powerful "shelter look" (as opposed to the sunshade look of H6, Longtail). This one looks like a good place to be during a rainstorm. Because the bracket is so prominent when seen from below it's important that the bracket, at least, be scribed to fit the siding or shingles of the wall. Remember, under the section on Poles and Posts, how the scribing technique was described? It's tricky when irregular posts are involved, but a zig-zag cut in a bracket is a snap.

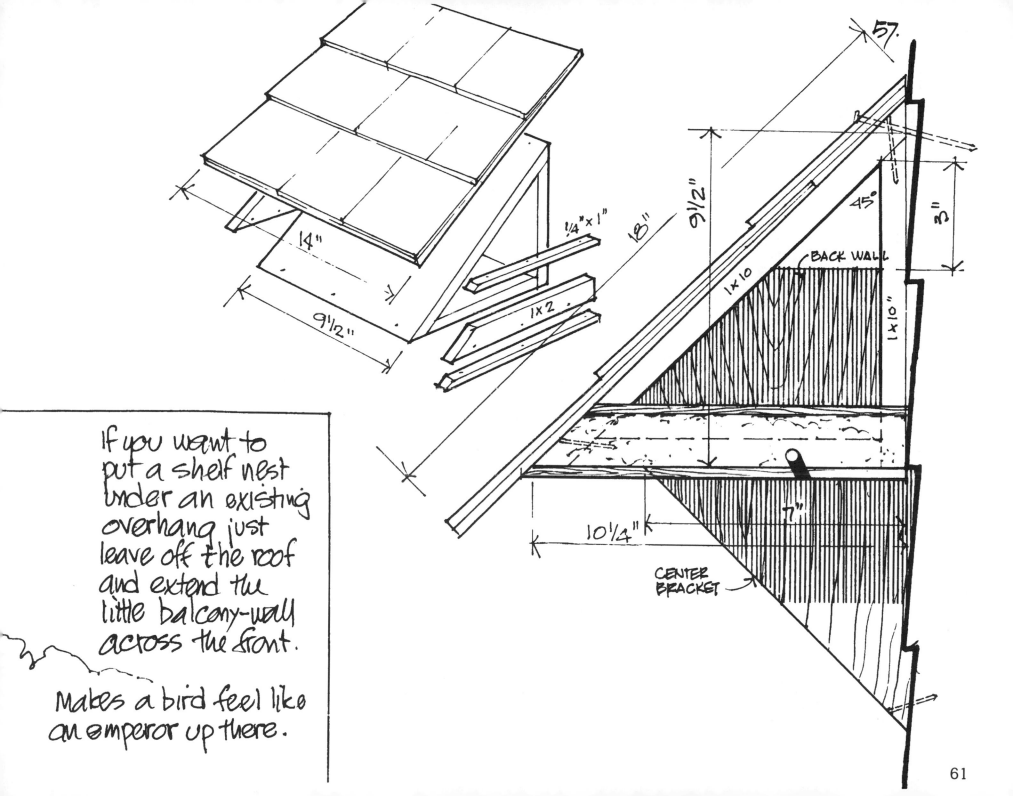

If you want to put a shelf nest under an existing overhang just leave off the roof and extend the little balcony-wall across the front.

Makes a bird feel like an emperor up there.

14"

9½"

¼"×1"

18"

1×2

57.

9½"

3"

45°

BACK WALL

1×10

1×10"

10¼"

7"

CENTER BRACKET

H8
The Wedge

You must be getting pretty good at all this by now. You can tell at a glance, I'll bet, that the removable roof of this birdhouse is held in place by 1) the weight of the 2" thick board atop the roof, plus 2) the 3/4" board on the underside that's cut to fit snugly inside the walls. You've noticed the 4 ventilation slots on each side, the drain opening at the bottom, the horizontal row of nails locating the floor, and the matching slopes of the roof and the perch.

So all you need are a few dimensions and you'll be on your way. The shapes are a little tricky but unless you try to miter all the odd-angle joints

REMEMBER THE TABLE ON PAGE 13 ! HOLE SIZE AND MOUNTING HEIGHT DETERMINE TYPE OF OCCUPANT.

you should have no trouble. Now I will cross my fingers and hope that the dimensions are right. If they aren't, well, I can offer you a refund on the book, or you could shave a bit here and cut a bit there until it all goes together.

Remember that no matter how proud you are to have this birdhouse, Mother Nature will want you to hide it among the leaves (where it and all man-made things belong).

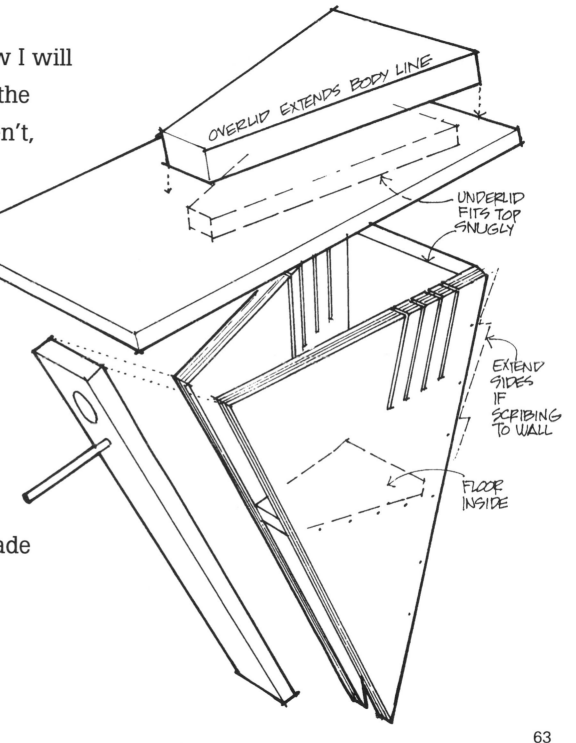

OVERLID EXTENDS BODY LINE

UNDERLID FITS TOP SNUGLY

EXTEND SIDES IF SCRIBING TO WALL

FLOOR INSIDE

This cross section is shown as if it were mounted against a flat wall. if the wall is not flat — if it is shingled or if it has beveled siding, all you need do, after you're 100% sure where you want to hang it, is to scribe and cut the overhanging side pieces as shown at left. This can be done after the birdhouse has been assembled.

Now, on to the cutting . . .

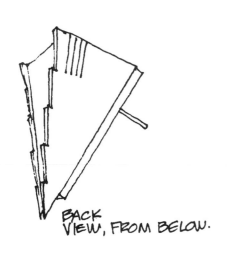

BACK
VIEW, FROM BELOW.

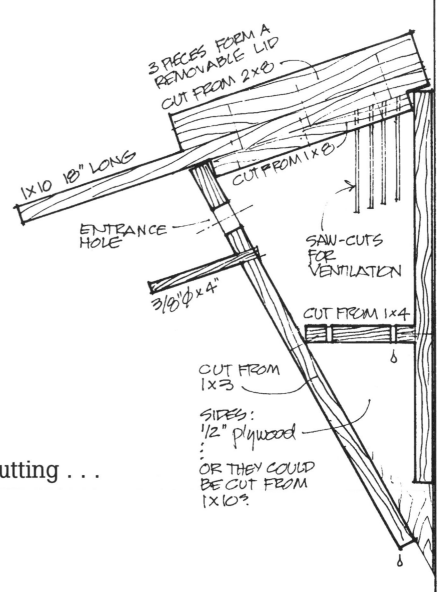

3 PIECES FORM A REMOVABLE LID CUT FROM 2×8

1×10 18" LONG

CUT FROM 1×8

ENTRANCE HOLE

SAW-CUTS FOR VENTILATION

3/8"∅×4"

CUT FROM 1×4

CUT FROM 1×3

SIDES: 1/2" plywood

OR THEY COULD BE CUT FROM 1×10?

Needed: <u>one</u> of each piece, except the 2 side pieces.

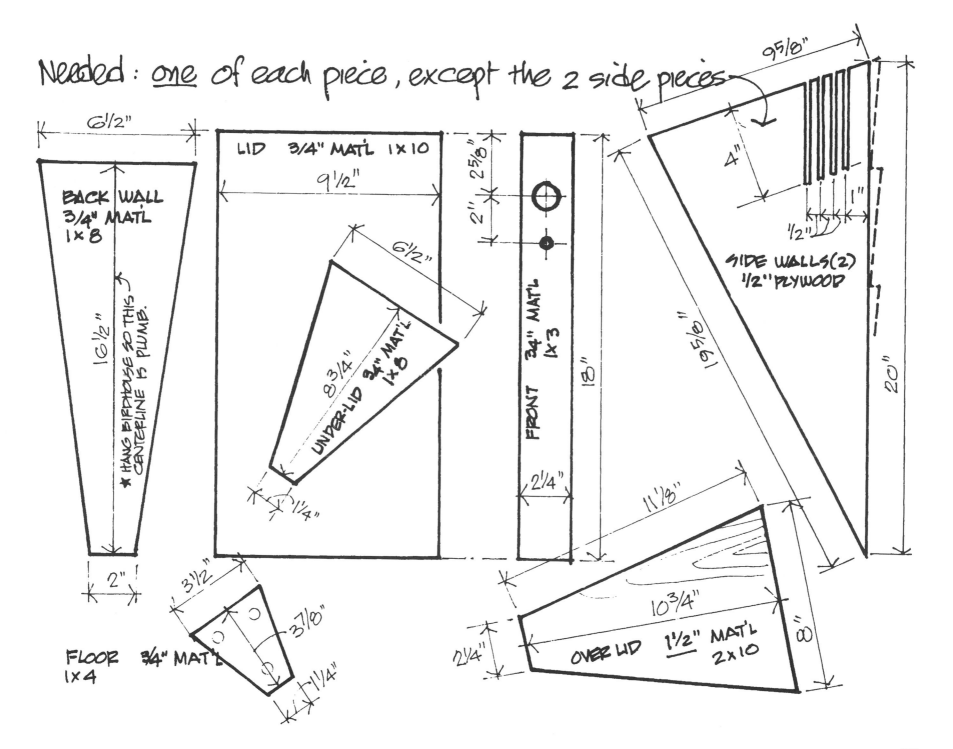

BACK WALL 3/4" MAT'L 1×8

★ HANG BIRDHOUSE SO THIS CENTERLINE IS PLUMB.

6½"

16½"

2"

LID   3/4" MAT'L 1×10

9½"

2"   2⅝"

UNDER-LID 3/4" MAT'L 1×8

6½"

8¾"

1¼"

FRONT 3/4" MAT'L 1×3

18"

2¼"

FLOOR   3/4" MAT'L 1×4

3½"

3⅞"

1¼"

9⅝"

4"

½"

1"

SIDE WALLS(2) 1/2" PLYWOOD

19⅝"

20"

11⅛"

10¾"

2¼"

8"

OVER-LID   <u>1½"</u> MAT'L 2×10

65

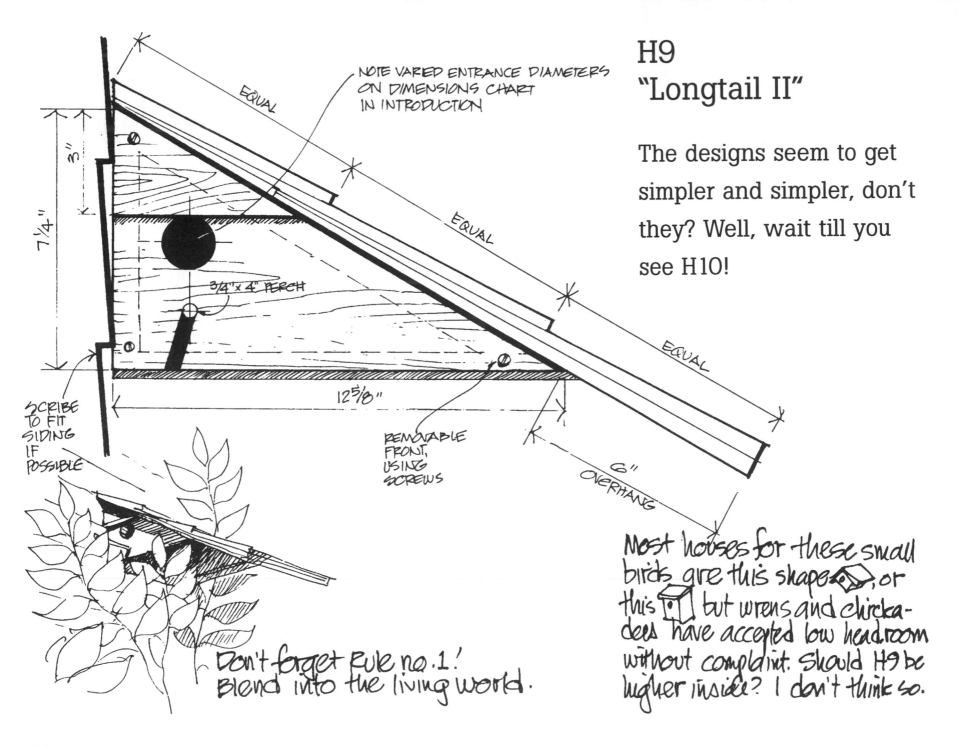

NOTE VARIED ENTRANCE DIAMETERS ON DIMENSIONS CHART IN INTRODUCTION

EQUAL

EQUAL

EQUAL

3"

7¼"

3/4" x 4" PERCH

SCRIBE TO FIT SIDING IF POSSIBLE

12⅝"

REMOVABLE FRONT, USING SCREWS

6" OVERHANG

H9
"Longtail II"

The designs seem to get simpler and simpler, don't they? Well, wait till you see H10!

Most houses for these small birds are this shape, or this but wrens and chickadees have accepted low headroom without complaint. Should H9 be higher inside? I don't think so.

Don't forget rule no.1! Blend into the living world.

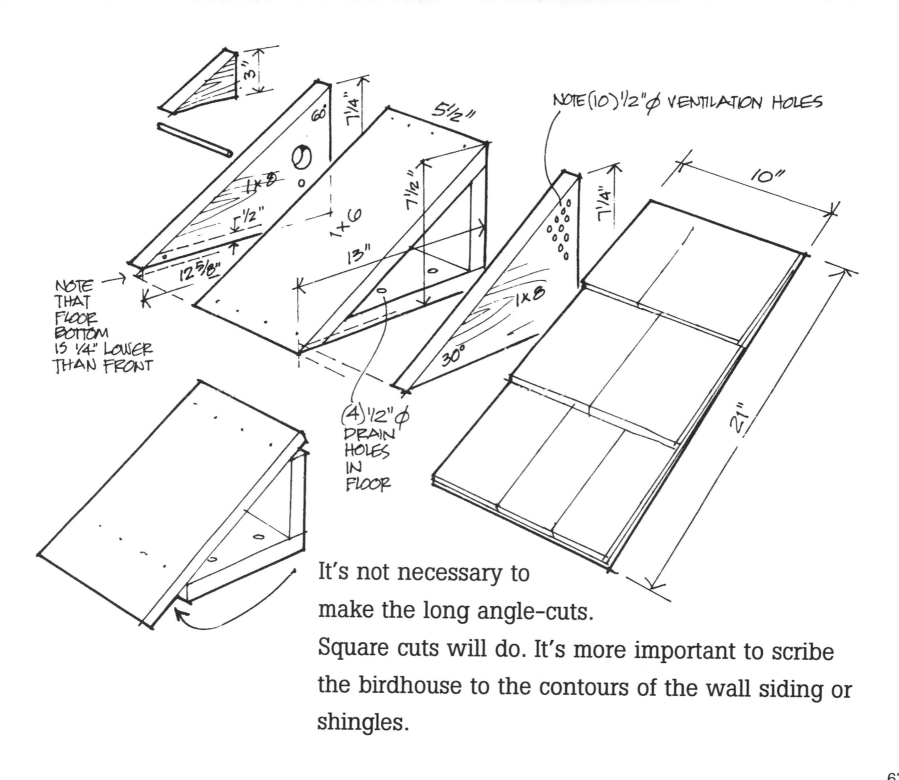

3"

60°

7¼"

5½"

NOTE (10) ½"∅ VENTILATION HOLES

1×8

½"

7½"

1×6

7¼"

10"

NOTE THAT FLOOR BOTTOM IS ¼" LOWER THAN FRONT

12⅝"

13"

1×8

30°

21"

(4) ½"∅ DRAIN HOLES IN FLOOR

It's not necessary to make the long angle-cuts.

Square cuts will do. It's more important to scribe the birdhouse to the contours of the wall siding or shingles.

H10
The Hangout

Wait!

Don't turn the page. It isn't as hard as it looks. And it doesn't look as complicated as you think. After you've looked at it a while you'll see that it's not confusing or complicated; it's simply unified.

If you're going to say "45 degrees" in a design, you don't want to do it hesitantly or everyone will be embarrassed. Say it with strength, and then carry it through into the details. It's what nature does with all the details. Look at any flower, any pine cone, any leaf. This is just a poor attempt to go all-out the way the living world does.

This is a simple 45° birdhouse with a few modifications.

First, I pulled one side down , then I elongated the roof on that side.

Next, I added a center fin, or vane, to act as a wall bracket.

Following that, I made the entrance square 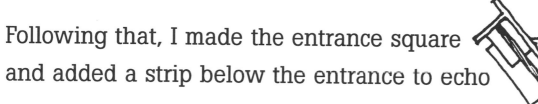 and added a strip below the entrance to echo the roof angle.

Then it was just a matter of perches and details.

That doesn't sound very bad, now, does it?

Even the square perches are easy. Simply carve their ends using a utility knife, and force them into the holes you've drilled.

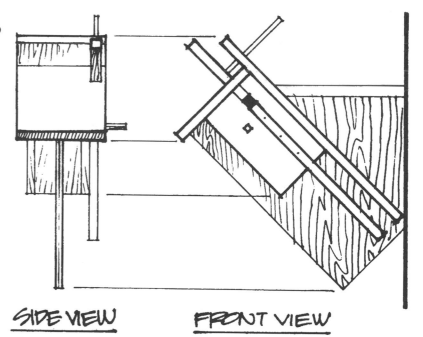

SIDE VIEW   FRONT VIEW

69

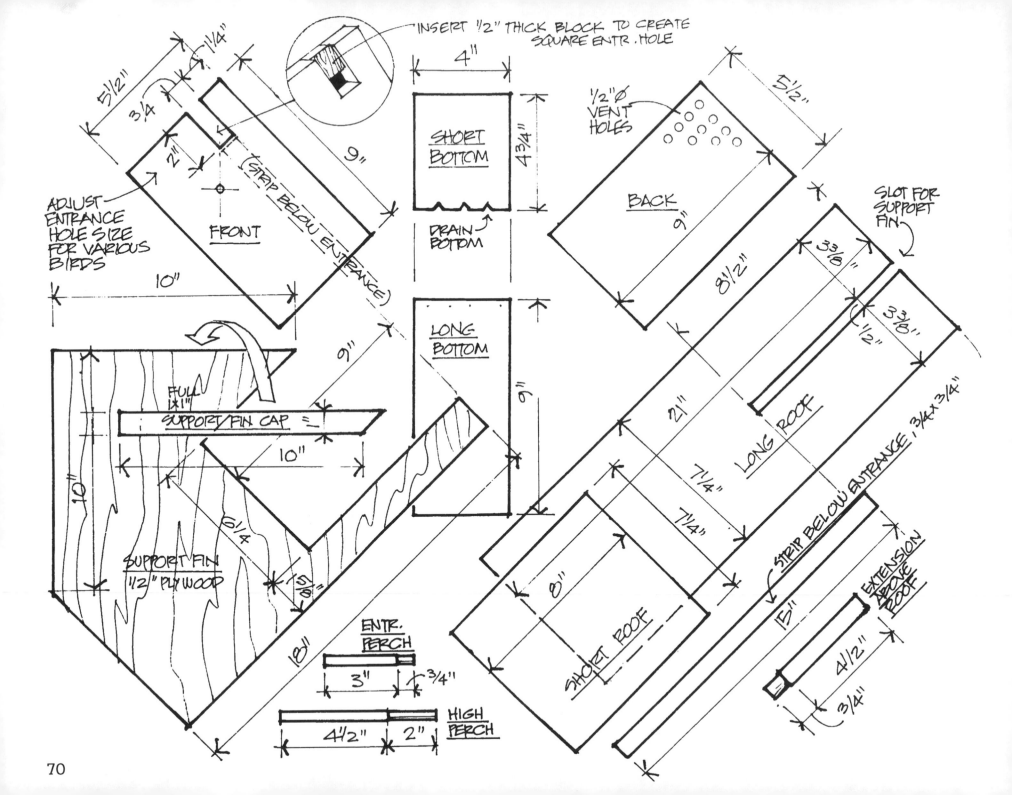

INSERT 1/2" THICK BLOCK TO CREATE SQUARE ENTR. HOLE

SHORT BOTTOM

4"

4¾"

DRAIN BOTTOM

FRONT

5½"

3/4

2"

1¼"

9

9"

(STRIP BELOW ENTRANCE)

ADJUST ENTRANCE HOLE SIZE FOR VARIOUS BIRDS

10"

1/2"∅ VENT HOLES

BACK
9"

5½"

8½"

SLOT FOR SUPPORT FIN

FULL 1×1"

SUPPORT/FIN CAP

10"

10"

6¼"

15/8"

SUPPORT FIN
1/2" PLYWOOD

18"

LONG BOTTOM

9"

9"

3⅜"

3⅜"

1/2"

2"

LONG ROOF

7¼"

7¼"

STRIP BELOW ENTRANCE 3/4 × 3/4

EXTENSION ABOVE ROOF

ENTR. PERCH

3"

3/4"

HIGH PERCH

4½"

2"

8"

SHORT ROOF

15"

4½"

3/4"

H11 The Pass-Through

This one must look like a snap compared to that chaotic scene at left, and it is a snap, just a simple variation of "The Hangout." Its main feature is a tail, made of 2x3 or 2x4, that appears to pass through the supporting post, and you're free to chip and chisel a tunnel through the post if you like, but a simpler and equally appealing way is simply to add a separate tail-stub on the other side of the post. Just don't do either one if the "post" happens to be a life tree. That would wound it unforgivably. If you must deal with a living tree then you should devise a hanging variation of this birdhouse that can make use of soft cords looped over a branch for support. Birds don't mind swaying a bit in the wind.

P.13 GIVES YOU THE HOLE SIZE AND MOUNTING HEIGHT FOR EACH BIRD'S HOUSE.

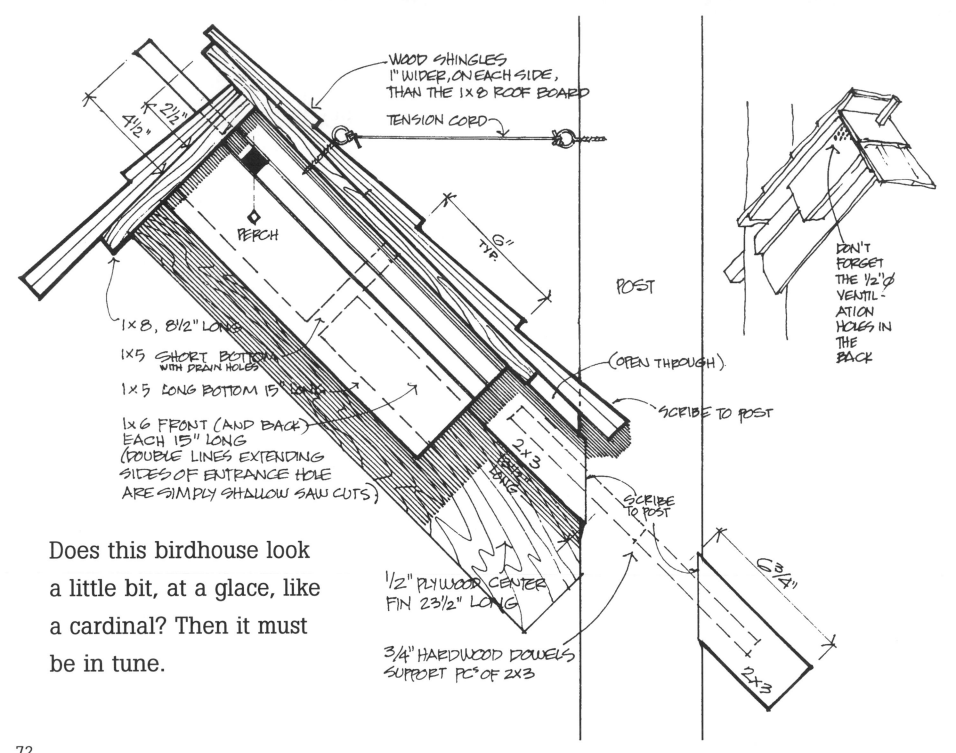

WOOD SHINGLES 1" WIDER, ON EACH SIDE, THAN THE 1x8 ROOF BOARD

TENSION CORD

PERCH

6" TYP.

POST

(OPEN THROUGH).

SCRIBE TO POST

DON'T FORGET THE 1/2"∅ VENTILATION HOLES IN THE BACK

1x8, 8½" LONG

1x5 SHORT BOTTOM WITH DRAIN HOLES

1x5 LONG BOTTOM 15" LONG

1x6 FRONT (AND BACK) EACH 15" LONG (DOUBLE LINES EXTENDING SIDES OF ENTRANCE HOLE ARE SIMPLY SHALLOW SAW CUTS)

2x3

23½" LONG

SCRIBE TO POST

6¾"

2x3

½" PLYWOOD CENTER FIN 23½" LONG

3/4" HARDWOOD DOWELS SUPPORT PCS OF 2x3

Does this birdhouse look a little bit, at a glace, like a cardinal? Then it must be in tune.

H12   The Skyscraper

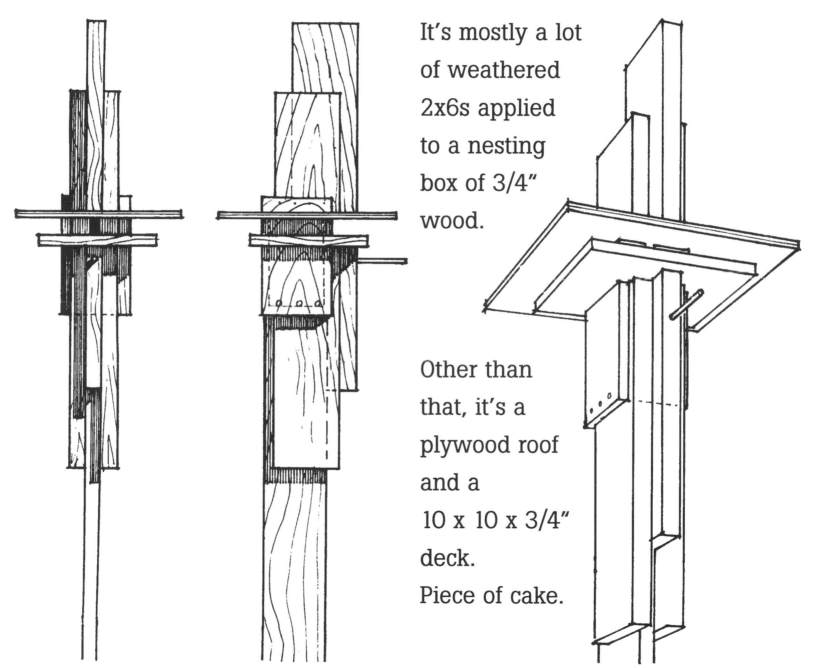

It's mostly a lot of weathered 2x6s applied to a nesting box of 3/4" wood.

Other than that, it's a plywood roof and a 10 x 10 x 3/4" deck. Piece of cake.

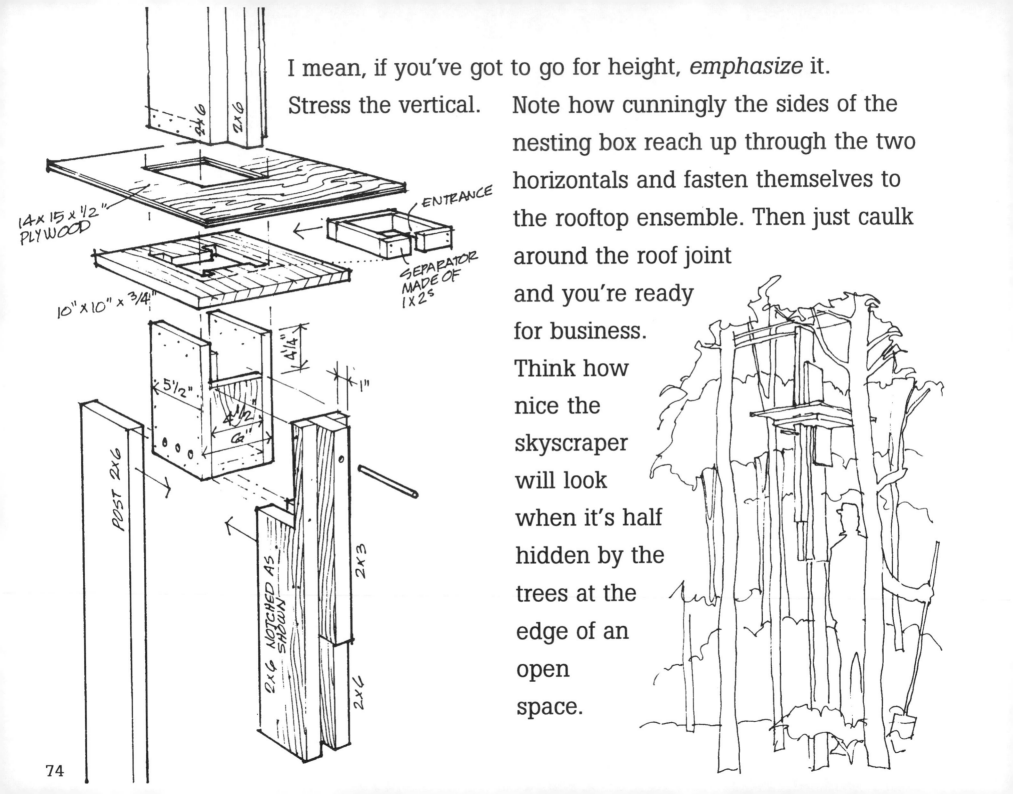

I mean, if you've got to go for height, *emphasize* it. Stress the vertical. Note how cunningly the sides of the nesting box reach up through the two horizontals and fasten themselves to the rooftop ensemble. Then just caulk around the roof joint and you're ready for business. Think how nice the skyscraper will look when it's half hidden by the trees at the edge of an open space.

2x6

2x6

14x15x½" PLYWOOD

ENTRANCE

SEPARATOR MADE OF 1X2s

10" X 10" X ¾"

4¼"

5½"

1"

4½"

6"

POST 2x6

2x6 NOTCHED AS SHOWN

2x3

2x6

H13
The Lattice House

I'd like to see if you can wing it alone with this one. You can hardly go wrong. Any similar design will only enhance the 45° theme. Just don't introduce any odd angles or take away the deep-shelter look.

Scale: 1/4" = 1 inch
(1/4 full size)

P.13 FOR HOLE SIZES, INTERIOR SPACE, ETC.

H14   The Condo

I've never been successful in attracting a pair of purple martins, let alone a colony of them, but then I've only had one season to try this design. Maybe they haven't found it yet. Or maybe they don't recognize this stunning piece of aerial architecture after all the years they've been exposed to the drab designs so typical of multi-family housing in the past.

Basically, all you need is a cluster of well-ventilated cubicles, each about 6" x 6" x 6", with 2" entrance holes. The birdhouse at left has 8 such cubicles, arranged in a tick-tack-toe # pattern with the center cubicle reserved for the post.

Because of the required 15-to-20-foot height of the house, a sturdy pole is essential.

If you can't tip the house up and down from the ground, be careful up there on the ladder! I don't want to lose a book customer.

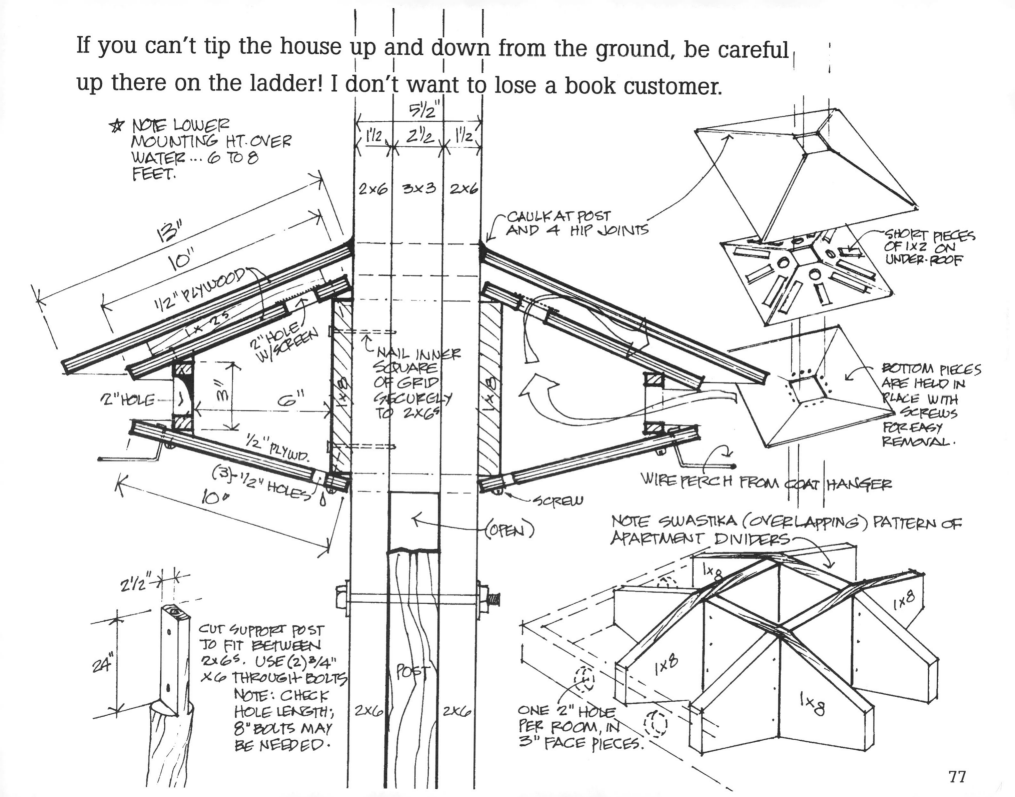

✱ NOTE LOWER MOUNTING HT. OVER WATER … 6 TO 8 FEET.

5½"

1½" 2½" 1½"

2x6 3x3 2x6

13"

10"

½" PLYWOOD

1 × 2s

2" HOLE W/SCREEN

2" HOLE

3"

6"

½" PLYWD.

(3) 1½" HOLES

10"

CAULK AT POST AND 4 HIP JOINTS

NAIL INNER SQUARE OF GRID SECURELY TO 2X6s

1×8

(OPEN)

SCREW

SHORT PIECES OF 1x2 ON UNDER·ROOF

BOTTOM PIECES ARE HELD IN PLACE WITH SCREWS FOR EASY REMOVAL.

WIRE PERCH FROM COAT HANGER

2½"

24"

CUT SUPPORT POST TO FIT BETWEEN 2X6S. USE (2) ¾" X6 THROUGH·BOLTS NOTE: CHECK HOLE LENGTH; 8" BOLTS MAY BE NEEDED.

POST

2x6   2x6

NOTE SWASTIKA (OVERLAPPING) PATTERN OF APARTMENT DIVIDERS

1×8

1×8

1×8

1×8

ONE 2" HOLE PER ROOM, IN 3" FACE PIECES.

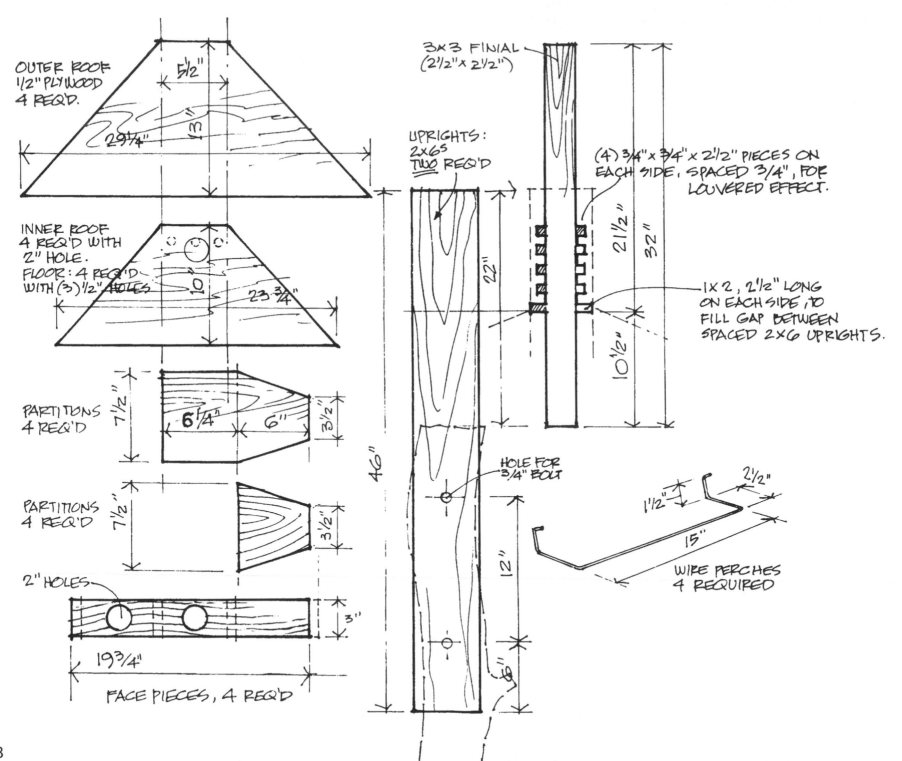

OUTER ROOF
1/2" PLYWOOD
4 REQ'D.

5½"

13"

29¼"

INNER ROOF
4 REQ'D WITH
2" HOLE.
FLOOR: 4 REQ'D
WITH (3) ½" HOLES

23 3/4"

PARTITIONS
4 REQ'D

7½"

6¼"   6"   3½"

PARTITIONS
4 REQ'D

7½"

3½"

2" HOLES

19 3/4"

FACE PIECES, 4 REQ'D

3x3 FINIAL
(2½" x 2½")

UPRIGHTS:
2x6s
TWO REQ'D

22"

46"

12"

6"

HOLE FOR
3/4" BOLT

(4) 3/4" x 3/4" x 2½" PIECES ON
EACH SIDE, SPACED 3/4", FOR
LOUVERED EFFECT.

21½"   32"

10½"

1x2, 2½" LONG
ON EACH SIDE, TO
FILL GAP BETWEEN
SPACED 2x6 UPRIGHTS.

2½"

1½"

15"

WIRE PERCHES
4 REQUIRED

78

I show on page 77 screen wire over the 2" vent holes in the inner roof. It's not there to keep bugs out; it's there to keep baby martins (marteenis?) from trying to get out that way and getting trapped between the roof layers.

Martins are said to prefer white painted houses. That's why I felt safe in suggesting a roof of cheap, thin, 1/2" plywood out in the fierce exposure to sunlight and rain. If you give all the exterior surfaces two good coats of a latex white paint made for exterior use, the plywood should last for several years before it needs repainting. Now, how do you make the transition from white paint to earthy natural wood (the color of the post)? Simple. Starting here at point X, begin to thin the paint more and more with water as you go below that point, so that by the time you're a foot or two down the post all the pigment has disappeared.

OPEN

✗

This top section is almost 5 feet long. It is awkward and heavy. Be careful lifting and erecting it!

H15
Hardball

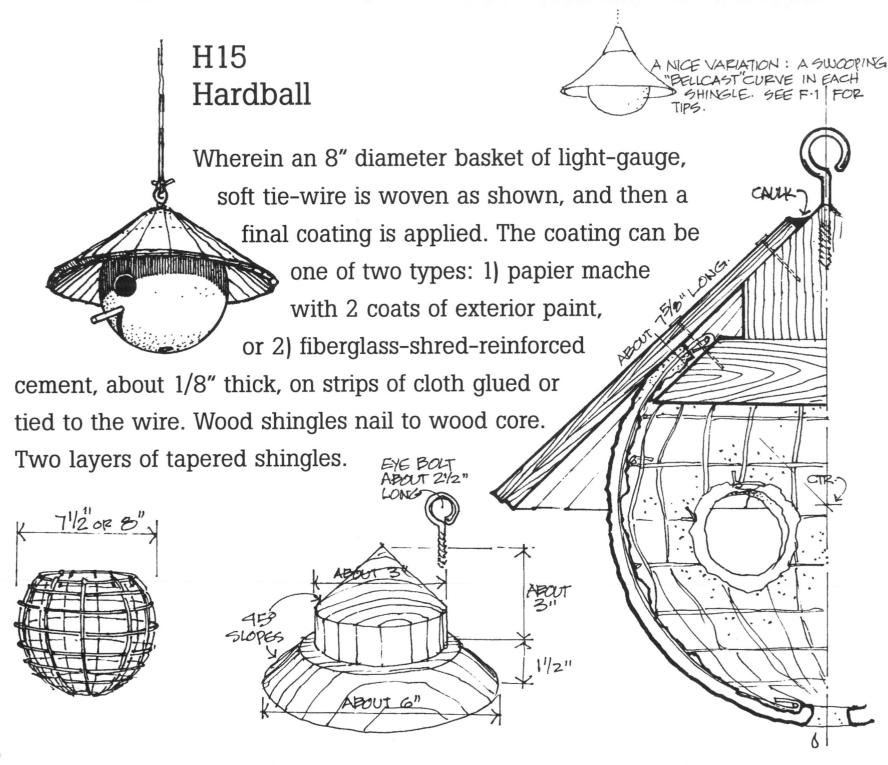

A NICE VARIATION: A SWOOPING "BELLCAST" CURVE IN EACH SHINGLE. SEE F·1 FOR TIPS.

Wherein an 8" diameter basket of light-gauge, soft tie-wire is woven as shown, and then a final coating is applied. The coating can be one of two types: 1) papier mache with 2 coats of exterior paint, or 2) fiberglass-shred-reinforced cement, about 1/8" thick, on strips of cloth glued or tied to the wire. Wood shingles nail to wood core. Two layers of tapered shingles.

CAULK

ABOUT 7 5/8" LONG

EYE BOLT ABOUT 2 1/2" LONG

CTR.

7 1/2" OR 8"

ABOUT 3"

45° SLOPES

ABOUT 3"

1 1/2"

ABOUT 6"

H16   The Shaft

They just get easier and easier, don't they? Well, they should; this is the last one: a birdhouse for any of the small birds you can accommodate using the dimensions in the table.* Octagon, 8 sides 45°.

(FULL-SIZE DETAIL)

3/4"

22 1/2°

A 1×3 WITH 22 1/2° SIDE-CUTS PROVIDES A 4 1/2" WIDE INTERIOR SPACE

A 1×4 WITH 22 1/2° SIDE - SLOPE CUTS PROVIDES AN INTERIOR SPACE 7" ACROSS

CUT 45° DOWNWARD SLOPE ON BOARD ABOVE ENTRANCE TO ACT AS A DRIP EDGE.

DRILL UPWARD-SLOPING 1/2"Ø HOLES FOR VENTS JUST BELOW NEST BOX CEILING.

RECESSED BOARD ALL THE WAY DOWN

THE CHOICE

FROM 2×6

1×3 FILLER RECESSED AT ENTRANCE SIDE

2 1/2"
1×3

FROM 2×8

1×4

3 1/2"
1×4

CUT 3/4" FROM ONE SIDE OF EACH HORIZONTAL PARTITION FOR RECESSED BOARD.

*P.13

F1
The Roundtable

Together, we have made it at last to the F-series, the feeders, of which there are only five, this one being my favorite. It hangs from the limb of a big old pitch pine by a soft rope.

Construction consists of little more than a series of pieces strung onto a 1/4" threaded rod (available at any building supply store) and a lot of tapered wood shingles nailed to two wood discs located in the attic.

DISCS OF WOOD

1/4" THREADED ROD

1 1/8 x 3/4" PIECES →

EDGE RAIL

3/4" PLYWOOD

YOU'LL PROBABLY HAVE TO SOAK THE 3/16" x 1 1/2" EDGE RAIL TO GET IT TO GO AROUND. TIE A ROPE AROUND IT WHILE IT DRIES.

WOOD SHINGLES

Threaded rods are made of fairly weak metal. After I'd slipped all the drilled pieces of wood onto the rod and nailed all the slim, tapered shingles into place, I found that by using a pair of pliers and my great sinewy arms I was able to curl the rod into a double loop before hacksawing off the excess length. Then it was simply a matter of adding the sheet metal cap and caulking it tight.

Now it's your turn to try it. I hope you'll enjoy it as much as I did.

The best way to handle the metal cap is to experiment with paper templates. Find the length (radius) and arc that fit best, then cut that shape out of metal. Wrap it around the top of the roof, tack it to the upper wood attic disc, and smear caulking into the top hole and the slit in the skirt. I used copper because it was available. If you use aluminum be sure to paint it a nice neutral color.

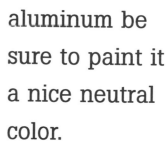

Use 1-1/2" diameter closet-pole wood for the center columns. Or use square wood and simply round the very top where the shingle tips rest.

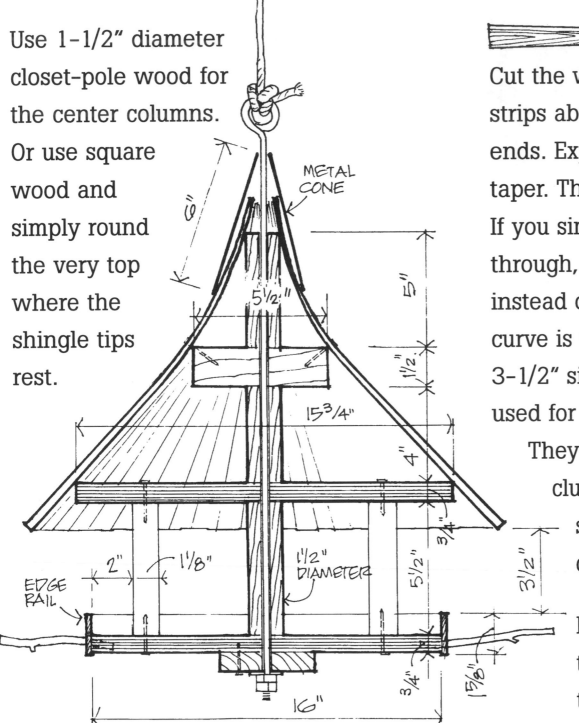

METAL CONE

8"

5½"

15¾"

5"

1½"

4"

¾"

2"

1⅛"

1½" DIAMETER

5½"

3½"

EDGE RAIL

16"

¾"

1⅝"

Cut the wood shingles into tapered strips about 1" wide at the butt ends. Experiment to get the right taper. Then pre-drill the nail holes. If you simply pound the nails through, the shingles may break instead of curve, and the sweeping curve is the key to this design. The 3-1/2" side opening dimension is used for positioning the shingles.

They'll make such a jagged clutter at the peak you'll soon see why the metal cap-cone is needed.

Note the double nuts below the floor. They lock tight that way.

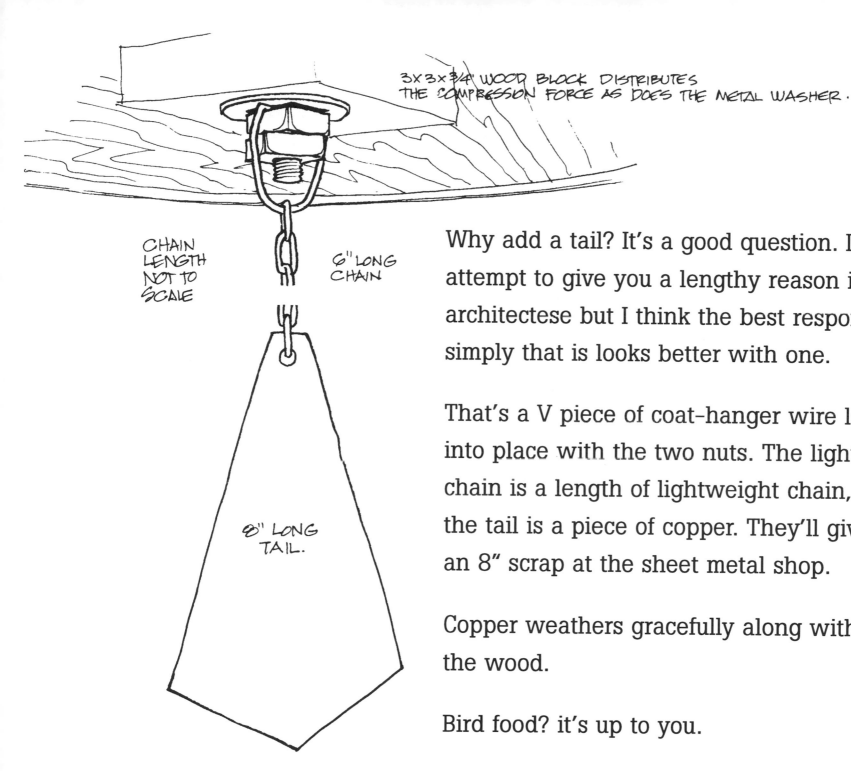

3×3×¾" WOOD BLOCK DISTRIBUTES THE COMPRESSION FORCE AS DOES THE METAL WASHER.

CHAIN LENGTH NOT TO SCALE

6" LONG CHAIN

8" LONG TAIL.

Why add a tail? It's a good question. I can attempt to give you a lengthy reason in architectese but I think the best response is simply that is looks better with one.

That's a V piece of coat-hanger wire locked into place with the two nuts. The lightweight chain is a length of lightweight chain, and the tail is a piece of copper. They'll give you an 8" scrap at the sheet metal shop.

Copper weathers gracefully along with the wood.

Bird food? it's up to you.

F2
Squirrel-Proof

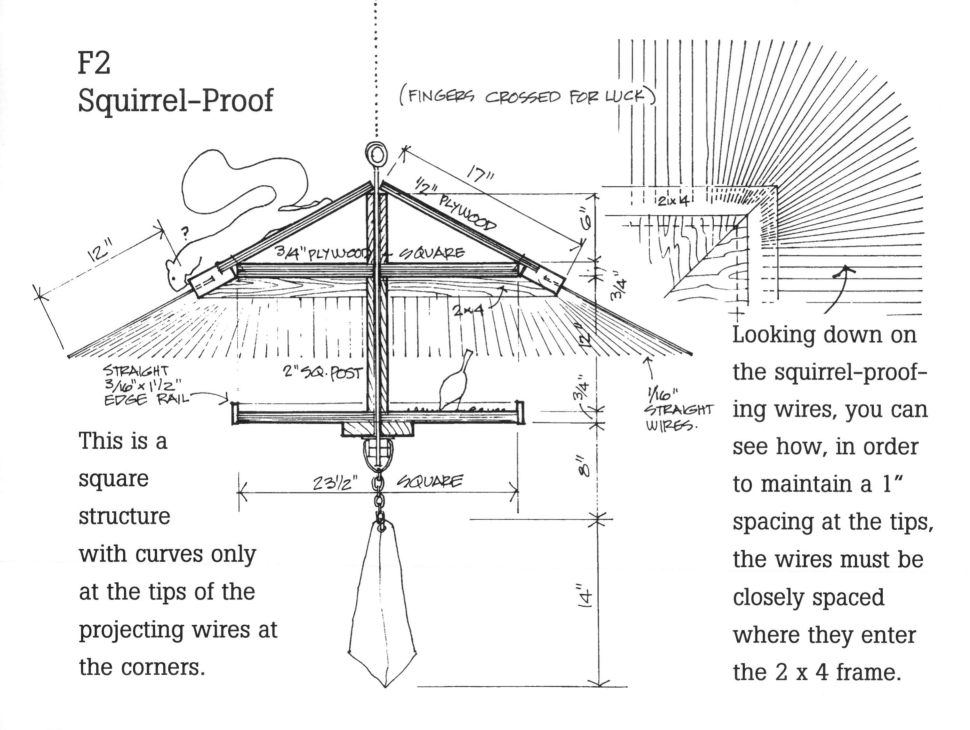

(FINGERS CROSSED FOR LUCK)

17"

1/2" PLYWOOD

3/4" PLYWOOD SQUARE

12"

?

6"

3/4"

2×4

12"

STRAIGHT
3/16" × 1 1/2"
EDGE RAIL

2" SQ. POST

2×4

1/16"
STRAIGHT
WIRES.

3/4"

8"

23 1/2"   SQUARE

14"

This is a square structure with curves only at the tips of the projecting wires at the corners.

Looking down on the squirrel-proofing wires, you can see how, in order to maintain a 1" spacing at the tips, the wires must be closely spaced where they enter the 2 x 4 frame.

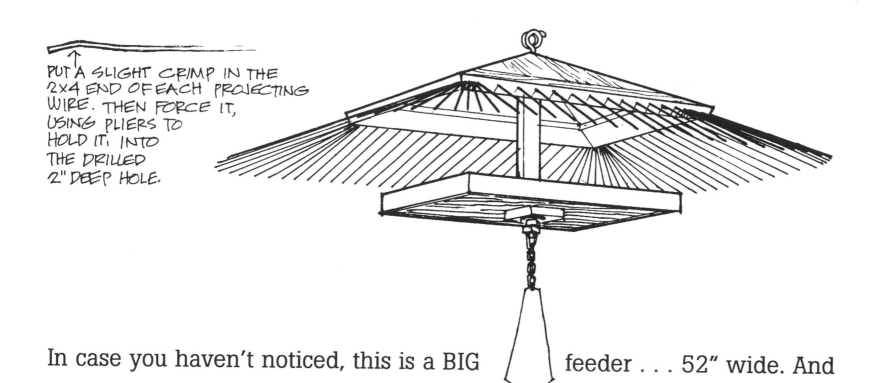

PUT A SLIGHT CRIMP IN THE 2×4 END OF EACH PROJECTING WIRE. THEN FORCE IT, USING PLIERS TO HOLD IT, INTO THE DRILLED 2" DEEP HOLE.

In case you haven't noticed, this is a BIG feeder . . . 52" wide. And ungainly, too, with all those wires sticking out of it. Don't get stabbed. And be sure to file smooth the edges of the sheet metal tail. Use soft rope if the feeder is to be hung from a living tree. Hang the feeder high enough from the ground (6 feet?) to discourage squirrel jumps.

Consider a pulley for lowering the feeder.

ROOF PIECE, TYPICAL OF ALL 4.

½" PLYWOOD

ENDS OF 2×4 EDGE FRAME MUST BE UNDERCUT (MITERED) FOR PIECES TO JOIN.

17"

31½"

2×4

½×1" RECESS IN 2×4 EDGE.

F3
The Flying Saucer

By now, you've probably gotten so good at building these feeders and birdhouses you need only a glance at my sketch to be on your way to the workbench, so I don't want to belabor the point. You're probably a better craftsman than I, too. At this point in our acquaintance I care only about the proportions, and it's a well-founded concern. I've seen too many good ideas go down the drain because of overlooked proportions. Some were just enough off to be painful looking; a few were so far off as to be almost funny.

Almost.

The birds don't care, of course, but we've already discussed that.

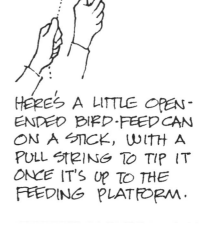

HERE'S A LITTLE OPEN-ENDED BIRD-FEED CAN ON A STICK, WITH A PULL STRING TO TIP IT ONCE IT'S UP TO THE FEEDING PLATFORM.

And what, you wonder, are those little things up on the spire, the ones that look a little like marshmallows on a stick? Well, I'd like to leave that up to you. They can be pairs of nuts locked together on the threaded rod. They can be little blocks of wood carefully threaded into place. Or they can be walnut shells carefully drilled and placed.

Try to carry the line of the roof up into a punctuated spire that really has the sweep of the one in the sketch over yonder. This feeder should appear to sit lightly on its support.

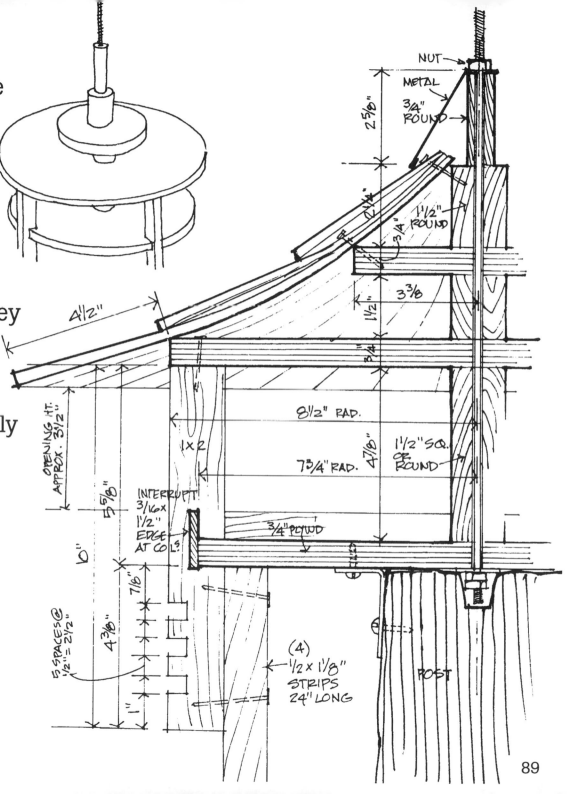

F4
The Hanging Saucer

All I did was substitute
a lower stem for the support
post. The catch is that that stem
must be drilled through from top to
bottom. And unless you own extension
bits you can't drill more than about 3 inches.
That's why you can see a joint at mid-stem:
it's in two pieces.

If it's well–proportioned, the hanging saucer will look as if it could rise
up and float away like a balloon.

F5
The Christmas Tree

I had to clap two boards together, just now, in order to chase the birds away. There were so many of them you couldn't see any of my workmanship. When tray after tray is filled, it drives birds into a kind of feeding frenzy. They seem to come from nowhere.

That can lead to two problems, one for the feeder (you) and one for the feedees. First, the enthusiasm of the birds on all those trays lends to great expenditures for seed, and second, the expenditures can lead to abandonment of the whole program in midwinter, just when the birds have become most dependent upon their human benefactors.

So don't get involved unless you're prepared to stay with it straight through the winter.

Now, as for the construction, it's just a series of trays made of 1 x 6's with little rails round them. The trays are supported on 1 x 3's which, as you can see, extend only about 2/3 of the way under the trays. And the 1 x 3's cantilever from the center post on dowels. Naturally, the dowels should be as large as possible. Half-inch ones are ideal. But you have to be mighty careful drilling 1/2" holes in 3/4" stock. There's little room to spare.

Proportions? Well, use your eye. Make the tray-tree graceful.

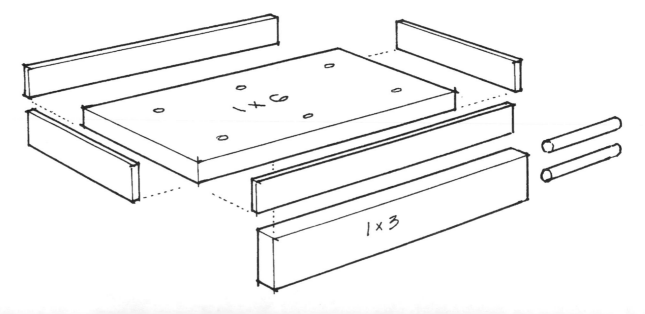

1 x 6

1 x 3

B1
The Earthbath

Now that you've graduated from birdhouses and feeders into the rarefied air of birdbaths, it's time to get your hands dirty. Now it's time for the most fun of all: casting big bowls of concrete, right in the earth.

You can imagine how it's done but there are a few tips worth offering so I might as well give you some step-by-step instructions. Then you won't make any of the mistakes I made.

You don't need a wheelbarrow or a mortar box. You can mix the cement on a big scrap piece of plywood. All you have to do is follow the mixing instructions on the label. The label is on a pre-mixed mortar available at your local building supply house. It's cheap, so why not buy 2 or 3 fifty-pound bags while you're at it? It's awful to run out of material when your birdbath is only half finished.

Remember that you're going to have to lift your masterpiece after it's cured, so don't make it too big. You may need a shovel — or a pick! — to loosen the earth. Here on Cape Cod I can do it with a garden trowel. Try to get 1) a true circle, and 2) a level rim. Keep scraping and filling and eyeballing your crater till you're satisfied with the shape. Then spray it gently till it's well soaked. If it's not wet it will pull all the water out of the mortar mix. Now go mix that cement!

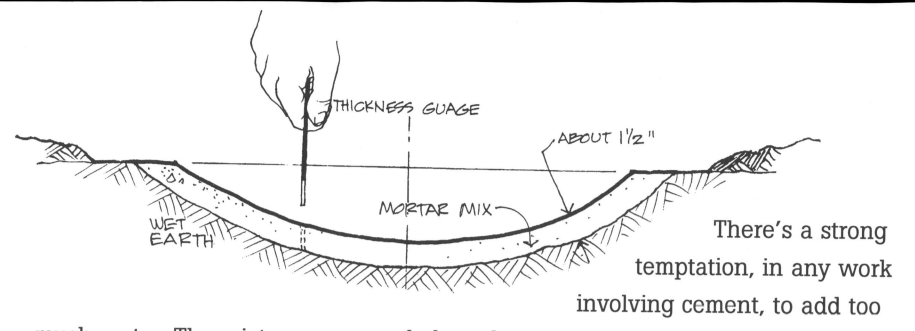

There's a strong temptation, in any work involving cement, to add too much water. The mixture seems to behave better when it's soft and wet but all the experts and all the rule books — and this architect — say the drier the better. Drier mixes produce stronger results with less shrinkage and cracking. Because they're on the solid, crumbly side, such mixes are hard to penetrate, so your depth gauge will have to be wiggled through the material. Once you have a more or less constant thickness all across the bowl, patch the test holes and start the cure! it starts with a cover-up. Carefully, so as not to jar or crack the new work, fill all the excavated earth back over it. Cement products must be damp-cured for at least seven days. That means wetting the cover-pile occasionally. Even after 7 days the bowl won't have its full strength. That will take 3 weeks.

They're telling me this is the last page so I'd better be brief: carefully exhume the cured bowl and set it on a bed of stiff mortar atop the post you've already erected for the stem. If the bowl is too heavy, that is if the mortar all gets squeezed out, start over with a supply of pebbles on hand, using them as either temporary or permanent shims while leveling the bowl. If you've mixed and cured the mortar right the bowl should ring when tapped. Still, it may be damaged by ice so try to keep it dry in bitter weather. (This is no bowl in which to provide lightbulb-heated water for the birds all winter.)

LEVEL

STIFF MORTAR MIX

BIG 10" - 12" POST (LOG)

KEEP THE ARRANGEMENTS GRACEFUL. LARGEST BOWL AT THE BOTTOM, LOTS OF PLANTS TO SOFTEN THE LEGGINESS. YOU'LL LOVE THEM.

Well, you're on your own, now. Good luck.

Happy birding.